lecting the great number of what were originally composite phonograms in the written language. Even in the case of composite ideograms it can be argued that these are no more than dead metaphors in the language, that a native speaker reading the Chinese character for "sincerity" no more sees a man standing by his word than an English speaker sees "of one growth," the original metaphor in the English word. But clearly there is room for both sides to maneuver here. It depends first of all on who is doing the seeing, and distinctions should be made between a poet and a speed-reader. James Liu, no admirer of Pound's handling of Chinese, nevertheless concedes that the radical of even a composite phonogram may in some cases retain some of its power, as in the character for "loyalty," which contains the "heart" radical (*The Art of Chinese Poetry*, p. 15). Calling attention to the roots buried in the etymologies of certain Chinese characters is only doing what poets and teachers have always done: enriching, expanding, deepening, and renewing the meanings of key words rather than letting them slide by as abstract mental counters.

Imagine some Saxon seeing a common flower, certain species of which close their white rays over the golden disk in the center when the sun sets. Having seen, he knew something about the flower, and having known, he named it: *dæges eage* ("the eye of day"). Centuries later the language of the Saxon was a dead language, incomprehensible to speakers of English, yet there was enough of a hint left in the name of the flower for poets to rediscover the power of that knowing, that naming:

> The longe day I shoop me for t'abide
> For nothing elles, and I shal nat lye,
> But for to loke upon the dayesie,
> That wel by reson men it calle may
> The "dayesye," or elles the "ye of day,"
> The emperice and flour of floures alle.

. . . .

111

> Whan that the sonne out of the south gan weste,
> And that this flour gan close and goon to reste
> For derknesse of the nyght, the which she dredde,
> Hom to myn hous ful swiftly I me spedde. . . .

More centuries later, the sounds of the language had changed beyond the point where this hint could be recognized in the name, but along comes William Carlos Williams, prompted by the poet Chaucer to recover again that old naming:

> The dayseye hugging the earth
> in August, ha! Spring is
> gone down in purple. . . .
>
> *(Collected Earlier Poems,* p. 208)

The second poet needed the first to teach him to see the day's eye in "daisy," for the written word in English represents the sound of the spoken word, and the spoken word has left its roots behind. Similarly, the written word "sincerity" represents a sound, and the English-speaker who does not delve back into Latin and reconstructed Indo-European has no hint of the roots of the word.[6] The visual form of the Chinese written character for "sincerity," however, continues to present to every reader who cares to see them the radicals "man" and "word" in a certain relationship, the root vision of sincerity as a man standing by his word. Such implications of meaning carried by the written character alone, regardless of how the word is pronounced, are impossible in alphabetic writing.

Pound's view of the ideogram, finally, is a heresy only if it is taken into the wrong church. He did not attempt to apply it to his *Cathay* translations, where he was following Fenollosa's careful crib. When he later began to use Chinese characters in *The Cantos* and in his Confucius translations, they were presented, even when the characters were simply dynastic names, as bold, complex forms emblematically set beside verses which involved and explored their enigmatic meanings. Pound's ideogram applies to poetics, to phanopoeia in the language of poetry, rather than to the particular discipline of Chinese poetry. It is, on a reduced scale, a juxtaposition of concrete elements just as Moritake's haiku and Pound's "The Return" juxtapose their images to create the phanopoeic structure of the poem, and it is nothing particularly new to poetics. Even when the radicals are not considered to be pictures of their meanings—and it was obvious to Pound that they often have no pictographic hint left—their combination in a composite ideogram can be seen as presenting a new, more complex meaning with the Image's sense of hard, clear particulars. "Sincerity" is presented not as an abstraction but as a structure of the visual (but not necessarily pictographic) elements "man" and "word" in a certain relationship. It is presented through the power of phanopoeia—a seen juxtaposition of visual elements, the generation of thought and meaning from that relationship, the containing of that relationship within a spatial form—and it gives the reader a single, new word.

The other direction these principles take, Pound's "ideogrammic method," is the same process on a larger scale. Hugh Kenner has discussed it fully in *The Poetry of Ezra Pound*, and it can be treated briefly here. The ideogram, operating on the level of the word, deals with the juxtaposition of elements within a single character. It appeared to Pound that in Chinese poetry the same principles operate on larger units as well, taking complete words or phrases and setting them beside one another without linking them through the explicit connections of grammatical prose. The lines of Ma Chih-yuan and Li Po, which do come over into literal English translation in just this way, are good examples of what Pound saw in Fenollosa's literal translations of Chinese poetry. It is a very short step from this to the juxtaposition of clearly seen objects, images, or feelings in the mind discussed in our previous chapter. This is the essence of the "ideogrammic method," though it can be further expanded to the juxtaposition of even larger units, of different historical consciousnesses, for example, as we find in *The Cantos*.

113

Pound's presentation of the ideogrammic method in the *ABC of Reading* begins:

> In Europe, if you ask a man to define anything, his definition always moves away from the simple things that he knows perfectly well, it recedes into an unknown region, that is a region of remoter and progressively remoter abstraction.
>
> Thus if you ask him what red is, he says it is a "colour."
>
> If you ask him what a colour is, he tells you it is a vibration or a refraction of light, or a division of the spectrum.
>
> And if you ask him what vibration is, he tells you it is a mode of energy, or something of that sort, until you arrive at a modality of being, or non-being, or at any rate you get in beyond your depth, and beyond his depth.

Pound conceived of the ideogrammic method as opposed to this way of thinking. It is a more "poetic" but no less rigorous mode of thinking based on the principles, by now familiar, of the juxtaposition of concrete images without conceptual interpretation:

> But when the Chinaman wanted to make a picture of something more complicated, or of a general idea, how did he go about it?
>
> He is to define red. How can he do it in a picture that isn't painted in red paint?
>
> He puts (or his ancestors put) together the abbreviated pictures of

> ROSE   CHERRY
>
> IRON RUST   FLAMINGO
>
> ·
>
> The Chinese "word" or ideogram for red is based on something everyone KNOWS. (pp. 5-9)

This is a somewhat garbled version of the material in Fenollosa's essay that is apparently Pound's source (*CWC*, p. 26). Fenollosa discussed how European logic moves from the concrete ("cherry") to the abstract ("redness"), but he did not say that Chinese, contemporary or ancestral, think as Pound says they do. Pound has again made something new, something that may not be true of Chinese thought but is a basic truth in poetic theory. (The primary Chinese character for "red" is itself a radical, though not a common one; rather than roses or flamingos its visual form suggests a relationship with the more common "fire" radical—but this is getting caught in Pound's own game.)

The ideogrammic method only brings to the surface a way of seeing that most readers of poetry already recognize. We can say the same things while remaining on more familiar ground, for the many "patterns of imagery" that have been discovered in all forms of literature are structures that work by means of the ideogrammic method. In addition to images, however, Pound's use of the method showed that larger units—particular voices out of Chinese or American history, mythological actions out of Homer or Ovid—would also function as elements of a particular pattern.[7] It is a method basic to phanopoeia's way of seeing, and to recognize it is not to deny that the complete poem, English or Chinese, may organize its language through conventional prose syntax as well.

Keats's ode "To Autumn" is a well-known example of a poem that does both. On one level, the "prose level" (as it is usually called), each of the three stanzas in the poem is a description. The first stanza describes the landscape of autumn with its loaded vines, bent apple trees, swollen gourds, plump hazel shells, and abundance of late flowers surrounded by bees; in the next stanza the activities of autumn are seen in the winnower, the reaper, the gleaner, and the cider-maker; in the final stanza the music of autumn is described in the sounds of the gnats, the bleatings of "full-grown lambs," and the songs of crickets, robins, and swallows. This, the poem tells us, is how autumn appears to the speaker. Yet as the reader moves through the poem from one stanza to the next he realizes that beneath this descriptive surface some kind of progression is taking place as well. The ripening into fruitfulness, almost overloaded fruitfulness, in the first stanza slows down in the second stanza into a sleepy exhaustion of both the land and man: the "careless" winnower resting on the granary floor, the reaper sleeping in the fields, the gleaner carrying her full basket homeward, and the patient cider-maker sitting and watching for hours the "last oozings" of the harvest. The last stanza brings the reader to endings, to stubbled fields, sunset, and swallows gathering to depart. He has not merely seen a description of autumn, he has moved with autumn through its changes. The poem, then, is also about time, about the transition from autumn to winter, though these things are not "said" by the speaker.

What is less clear in Pound's formulation of the ideogrammic method is that it involves the power of phanopoeia to catch time in spatial form. Time passes in Keats's autumn landscape, but phanopoeia also has the power to "make-things-present" by transforming the poem's progression of imagery into patterns of imagery, catching up and holding time and action as "red" could be caught and named in the simultaneous pattern of rose/cherry/iron rust/flamingo. The movement from mellow fruitfulness to empty fields has been superimposed upon another progression in the poem from morning mists through the harvest day to sunset, similar to the manner in which different cycles of maturity and decline are superimposed in the emblems of Quarles' *Hieroglyphics of the Life of Man.* And when the reader of "To Autumn" reaches the sunset, the stubbled fields, and the gathering swallows of the last stanza he must still see the morning mists and maturing fruitfulness of the first stanza and the exhausting harvest day of the second; otherwise he will be left with an autumn of endings only and not with the full naming of autumn that Keats gives. Time is caught in the pattern of a spatial form, in the ideogrammic method which is one of the poem's ways of knowing about autumn.

We have already seen other uses of this method. The three quatrains of Shakespeare's Sonnet 73 progress not through time but through images of diminishing scale which focus down from an autumn to a twilight to a dying fire, from the scale of a year to that of a day to the last hour or so of glowing embers. Blake's "Tyger," on the other hand, moves up through a widening pattern. The images of the blacksmith and his forge are set over the heart and brain of the Tyger; then this complex is set beside the images of the capitulating stars; the new complex is set beside the creation of the Lamb of Innocence, and all placed beneath the mysteriously smiling creator. In "The Inlaid Harp" Li Shang-yin set his vision of his transformed harp strings in a perspective of mythic patterns of metamorphosis, and Yeats in "The Magi" placed his momentary vision in the mythic pattern of a sacred quest worn down by time; the spatial form of both poems, I suggested, is that of an integrated curve. In all these poems the spatial pattern exists beneath, or above, or outside, the formal articulations of the prose meanings (though sometimes the pattern will break into these articulations and take control, leaving the incomplete, drunken sentence of Keats's first stanza or the fragmented interrogatives of Blake's poem). Within the patterns, phanopoeia is at work creating spaces for fuller knowing. In "To Autumn" temporal progression is caught in spatial pattern: a certain movement of time, a certain curve of natural cycles, is named. In Shakespeare's sonnet a dwindling down and a focusing down are caught in spatial pattern: the movements of a man's aging are named. In "The Tyger" hierarchical movement is caught in spatial pattern: creation is named.

When we turn from Pound to Fenollosa we encounter a writer who was both more precise and more speculative about his vision of Chinese writing and what it contributes to poetic theory. The precisions in *The Chinese Written Character as a Medium for Poetry* come from a working knowledge of Chinese, but the speculations finally derive from nothing more exotic than Emerson. The structure of this essay is tight and coherent, and its views can easily be distorted by being lifted out of context. Fenollosa did, for example, point several times to the pictographic hints in many Chinese characters, but not for the purpose of implying that the Chinese written language is picture-writing. Like Pound, Fenollosa was particularly interested in the structure of the composite ideogram. In the text of his essay and again in the appendix (which Pound gathered from Fenollosa's rough notes and added to the book in 1936) we see the suggestion that the character for "spring" is made up of the "sun" character placed beneath a character representing the bursting forth of plants, and that a character for "male" can be seen as a combination of "rice-field" and "struggle" (*CWC*, pp. 10, 38-39). In showing this, however, Fenollosa was not proposing a "split-character heresy" but was offering possible analogies of his central topic, which is action.

Fenollosa's views emphasized possibilities in poetic language that are somewhat different from what Pound later made of them. On both the level of the individual word and the level of the sentence or line of poetry Fenollosa was concerned with the active forces and movements carried by language. All languages, he felt, have actions at their roots. Every part of speech—a noun, an adjective, even a preposition—has an active verbal basis. Similarly, all sentences are at root transitive sentences, expressing the transference of forces from subject to object. Behind his theory stands a basically Emersonian assumption that language is "natural" rather than arbitrary, that it reflects basic structures and processes in nature. It was not a new view of language, but Fenollosa added to it the particular possibilities of visual, spatial form that he discovered in the Chinese written language. He saw both the individual ideogram and the ideogrammic sentence as containing within their visual forms fundamental actions and processes of the mind and of nature.

Considering the individual word, Fenollosa suggested that even in its pictographic beginnings the Chinese written language represents pictures not of things but of actions. "A true noun, an isolated thing, does not exist in nature. Things are only the terminal points, or rather the meeting points, of actions, cross-sections cut through actions, snapshots. Neither can a pure verb, an abstract motion, be possible in nature. The eye sees noun and verb as one: things in motion, motion in things, and so the Chinese conception tends to represent them" (p. 10). We have already seen how in Chinese the same word can function as either a noun or a verb. "Noun" and "verb," Fenollosa felt, are later categorizations which divide a more basic reality that includes both. Phanopoeia's power of seeing is in Fenollosa focused not simply on objects but on a more complex entity involving both objects and actions. He argued that the etymology of any language, if it is pushed back far enough, would reveal this active basis of the language. "In all languages, Chinese included, a noun is originally 'that which does something,' that which performs the verbal action. Thus the moon comes from the root *ma*, and means, 'the measurer.' The sun means that which begets" (p. 19; he is of course referring to the English words here). Since there are no negatives in nature, positive force being required to annihilate, this is reflected in language, and Fenollosa suggested that the English word "not," akin to the Sanskrit *na*, may have come from an Indo-European root *na* ("to be lost, to perish"). Copulative verbs are truncated active verbs: " 'Is' comes from the Aryan root *as*, to breathe. 'Be' is from *bhu*, to grow" (p. 15). It is tempting to dismiss Fenollosa's etymologies, in Chinese as well as English, as incidental to his theory, a left-over subservience to the nineteenth-century's view of language and its excitement over the discovery of Sanskrit. But they are not. Accurate

119

and inaccurate, they are serious attempts to plunge to what would now be called "deep structures" in language. Like spatial and temporal form in literature, the separation of nouns and verbs in grammar corresponds to an older science's view of nature; Fenollosa's "things in motion, motion in things" closes this separation, allowing the language of poetics to catch up with the language of science.

It might seem paradoxical that Pound took his highly visual ideas of the ideogram and the ideogrammic method from a treatise on poetic language in which the central topic is action. Yet there is no paradox in this, and no simple misreading of Fenollosa's words. As we saw in his Image poems, Pound, unlike Williams, does not explicitly trace the forces set up by his juxtapositions. He focuses on the clearly seen images rather than the energies of their relations, yet those energies are importantly there. In Fenollosa, the juxtaposition of elements within the composite ideogram is the naming of an action. The nouns "spring" and "male" are seen through their ideograms as actions: the energy of the sun pushing up the growing plants is a naming of spring; active struggle with the rice-field is a naming of "male." As in the composite ideogram for "home," the pig under the roof, these characters are compounds of discrete elements actively involved in a certain relationship. "In this process of compounding," Fenollosa wrote, "two things added together do not produce a third thing but suggest some fundamental relation between them" (p. 10).

The original compounding process that still continues to present the concept of sincerity as a man standing by his word led Fenollosa to affirm that the formation of such characters derives from the same roots that produce the metaphors of poetry. Every language, he felt, moved from the simple imitation of natural processes to more complex thought by means of metaphor, "the use of material images to suggest immaterial relations" (p. 22). In Chinese, traces of this archaic process are still recorded in the written characters. What was originally seen in those archaic metaphors, moreover, were actions. Once more Fenollosa appeals to the imitation of nature: since in nature forces and relationships are "more real" than objects, a metaphor is an imitation of an action:

> The whole delicate substance of speech is built upon substrata of metaphor. Abstract terms, pressed by etymology, reveal their ancient roots still embedded in direct action. But the primitive metaphors do not spring from arbitrary *subjective* processes. They are possible only because they follow objective lines of relations in nature herself. Relations are more real and more important than the things which they relate.
>
> (p. 22)

The fundamental roots of language lie in metaphor, and poetry can retrace these roots. "Metaphor, the revealer of nature, is the very substance of poetry. The known interprets the obscure, the universe is alive with myth" (p. 23). But since a metaphor is built on seeing an action, and is a mimesis in language of an active relationship in nature, poetry is also built on the imitation of natural actions, processes, relationships. Metaphor, the "chief device" of poetry, Fenollosa goes on to say, "is at once the substance of nature and of language. Poetry only does consciously what the primitive races did unconsciously. The chief work of literary men in dealing with language, and of poets especially, lies in feeling back along the ancient lines of advance" (p. 23).

At this point it should be clear that Fenollosa was saying what many others have said independently: Owen Barfield's *Poetic Diction* (1928) is another important statement of the same idea, but it runs back through the nineteenth and eighteenth centuries in the theories of Emerson, Max Müller, and Vico. According to this view all languages were to a significant degree built up from metaphor, and for Fenollosa the most vital activity of the poet lies in rediscovering this ancient language. It was a more "poetic" language than our present marketplace tongues, and at the same time it more accurately reflected truths about nature. The Chinese language has been left some distance behind as Fenollosa enters a more speculative realm in which Chinese is only a source of analogies for his theory of an ideal poetic language. He sees nature—and language, the reliable image of nature—as alive and active with forces and relationships, things being only the limits of action. The ideal poet, using the ideal poetic language, effortlessly recreates these forces and relationships. The real poet, using a real language, does what he can: "The more concretely and vividly we express the interactions of things the better the poetry. We need in poetry thousands of active words, each doing its utmost to show forth the motive and vital forces" (p. 28).

For the real poet, a written character offers unique possibilities, and in these lies the importance of the Chinese character to Fenollosa's theory of poetic language. Unlike words represented phonetically, some Chinese characters carry their etymologies, their metaphorical roots, visibly. Fenollosa gave one tantalizing example of the possibilities of character-writing when he suggested that a poet could repeat visual forms just as he is accustomed to repeating sounds in rhyme. It is, in fact, the same principle: "Poetry surpasses prose especially in that the poet selects for juxtaposition those words whose overtones blend into a delicate and lucid harmony. All arts follow the same law; refined harmony lies in the delicate balance of overtones." The harmonies of rhyme make us conscious of word-sounds we usually ignore. Similarly, in the simple, and scarcely poetic, Chinese line "The sun rises in the east," the visual forms of the characters contain exciting possibilities for phano-poeia-rhymes:

日   昇   東
Sun   Rises (in the) East

Fenollosa interprets the line:

122

The overtones vibrate against the eye. The wealth of composition in characters makes possible a choice of words in which a single dominant overtone colors every plane of meaning. . . . The sun, the shining, on one side, on the other the sign of the east, which is the sun entangled in the branches of a tree. And in the middle sign, the verb "rise," we have further homology; the sun is above the horizon, but beyond that the single upright line is like the growing trunk-line of the tree sign. (pp. 32-33)

If we discuss only "harmony," we have uncontroversial ornamentation, the characters acting to the eye as rhymes do to the ear. But rhyme in poetry has a way of moving beyond ornamentation, a way of discovering significant connections between the meanings of the rhyming words. Similarly here: Fenollosa's entire discussion has implied the far more interesting, if heretical, possibility that the visual overtones are not merely ornamental but do something with the meanings of the words. If not in Chinese then in his ideal poetic language poets can catch up the "motive and vital forces" of metaphorical relationships. In this short Chinese line, the "sun" radical is already part of the visual characters for "rise" and "east," reflecting, Fenollosa would say, an active part for the sun in the original metaphorical definitions of the *meanings* of "rise" and "east." Each character, then, contains within its deep archaic roots the action of the whole sentence—a resonance any poet would welcome.

When Fenollosa looked from the individual word to the larger unit of the sentence, he found that his basic assumption—language imitates the active forces and relationships in nature—applied here as well. The form of the sentence, he wrote, is mimetic of natural processes, and because of this the basic form is that of the transitive sentence. This form derives from the fact that natural phenomena are basically successive operations, the transference of force from agent

123

to object. Therefore language and thought, which follow nature, are successive also. An apparently intransitive sentence is actually a truncated representation of a transitive action: "He runs (a race)." "The sky reddens (itself)." "We breathe (air)." Similarly, there are no sentences that merely describe states rather than acts: "Who can doubt that when we say 'The wall shines,' we mean that it actively reflects light to our eye?" (pp. 13-14).

Once again, however, Fenollosa's theory gives us action within a visual form. Chinese writing, through the involvement of its visual characters, can reflect these operations of nature in a way that the arbitrary signs of phonetic writing cannot: "Chinese notation is something much more than arbitrary symbols. It is based upon a vivid shorthand picture of the operations of nature." A man sees a horse:

人	見	馬
Man	Sees	Horse

In the Chinese notation, Fenollosa said, characters can be selected that will follow natural suggestion: "First stands the man on his two legs. Second, his eye moves through space: a bold figure represented by running legs under an eye, a modified picture of an eye, a modified picture of running legs, but unforgettable once you have seen it. Third stands the horse on his four legs" (p. 8). As in "The sun rises in the east," the characters in this sentence rhyme visually, each character containing some indication of "legs." More important, however, is the way the characters vividly present the action of the seeing as it drives through the sentence from the subject ("man") to the object ("horse"). The sequential operations of nature, Fenollosa is saying, can be imitated either by sound-sequences or by image-sequences, and the sentence "Man sees horse" presents an action whether it is spoken or read. If it is read in his character-notation, however, it presents the action again, to the eye, with the temporal nature of the action caught in the spatial juxtaposition of visual characters. In this short sentence we see once again, then, a "progression of images" which, under another aspect, becomes pattern.

We began our investigations with the assumption that the roots of lyric are in language, and that phanopoeia is one power that charges these roots. Theories of phanopoeia in poetry, however, generally tend to shuttle back and forth between two conceptions of this power. One conception emphasizes creation, while the other conception involves perception and cognition. The first sees phanopoeia as primarily *poiesis*, a "making" that arises from the poet's doodling among the visual and structural possibilities in language. The second sees this radical power as primarily mimesis, an "imitation" or presentation in language of something that has been seen and known. The two conceptions go together, of course, and the poem, as Aristotle knew, is both mimesis and *poiesis*. It is, in Williams' words, "not 'like' anything but transfused with the same forces which transfuse the earth—at least one small part of them." In Fenollosa both conceptions of phanopoeia, creation and perception, are clearly accounted for.

"My subject is poetry, not language," he wrote, "yet the roots of poetry are in language" (*CWC*, p. 6). And the roots of language? His fundamental position is that the roots of language lie in the world and how we see it. Fenollosa's vision of language is expressed entirely in terms of the complex power of phanopoeia, and he traces that power back to find it rooted in nature. The poem is a *poiesis*, a creation out of language, but at a deeper level it is even more a mimesis. That is why clear seeing is necessarily the first step toward charging language with phanopoeia. The power does not simply mirror nature, however, for there are transformations involved as seeing becomes knowing, and again as knowing becomes naming. Fenollosa's idea of language is finally this: the processes and structures of nature are the roots of language, but only the roots; from these

roots language developed its own complex structures; finally, language arranges nature by structuring our seeing of it.
In a poet's hands, this is not simply an imaginary structuring of nature by an arbitrary language but a rediscovery
of nature through the natural roots still buried in language.
Language can structure the world as well as it does because
the world once structured language.

These archaic structures in language, Fenollosa said, are
structures of metaphor. The archaic metaphors through
which language was built up were modeled on the observed
world, and they are "at once the substance of nature and
of language." And again:

> This is more than analogy, it is identity of structure.
> Nature furnishes her own clues. Had the world not
> been full of homologies, sympathies, and identities,
> thought would have been starved and language chained
> to the obvious. (p. 22)

> Our ancestors built the accumulations of metaphor
> into structures of language and into systems of thought.
> Languages today are thin and cold because we think
> less and less into them. (p. 24)

A poet's "makings" consist of "feeling back along the ancient lines of advance." Sincerity is rediscovered as a man
standing by his word, and the daisy is seen again as the eye
of day.

Although Fenollosa would have objected to this, we
can see now that those ancient lines of advance stem not
from Archaic Chinese or from languages of "the primitive
races" but from a vision of Adam's namings in the Garden.
A seventeenth-century version of this vision of language
comes in Book VIII of *Paradise Lost* when Adam tells Raph-
ael of the effortless gift of naming he possessed upon first
awaking in Eden:

> . . . to speak I tri'd, and forthwith spake,
> My Tongue obey'd and readily could name

What e're I saw. Thou Sun, said I, fair Light,
And thou enlight'n'd Earth, so fresh and gay. . . .

And when God brought to him every beast of the field and
every fowl of the air:

I nam'd them, as they pass'd, and understood
Thir Nature, with such knowledge God endu'd
My sudden apprehension. . . .

In Milton's view it was the Fall, in Fenollosa's view simply
the thinning effects of time, that broke these immediately
apprehended correspondences between nature and language,
between seeing and knowing and naming. Poets now must
struggle with language to recover something of those correspondences. Fenollosa's Edenic model of the development
of language through metaphor, and the subsequent decline
in understanding this language, has long since been dis-
carded. It remains, however, a valuable model of the power
of phanopoeia in poetry, the seeing and knowing and naming that an individual poet follows as he structures his poetry
with the riddles, emblems, Images, and ideograms we have
been finding at the roots of lyric. Metaphor is one more
manifestation of this power. Language, as Fenollosa saw it,
still carries Eden in its roots, and our doodles in language
release these roots. Metaphor is "the revealer of nature" in
which, as in the riddle and the emblem, "the known interprets the obscure." It continues to be a naming, a rediscovery and a re-cognition of both language and nature.

Fenollosa's view of metaphor brings to a conclusion our
discussion of phanopoeia. The discussion has ranged con-
siderably beyond Pound's initial definition of phanopoeia
as "a casting of images upon the visual imagination," but it
has followed directions that he pointed out and has not in-
tentionally perverted them. Metaphor is a design, or configuration—a "figure" of speech—and only minor transformations are needed to see that it is simply the most familiar
of the structures in poetic language that derive from the

power of phanopoeia. At the roots, there are no essential differences between metaphor and the "hieroglyphics and enigmas" which to Wordsworth were later corruptions of the earliest poets' language of natural excitement. The riddle can be seen as a metaphor with one term concealed, and solving the riddle is a seeing into something that leads to a way of knowing. The ideograms which Fenollosa saw reflecting the metaphorical bases of language stand very close to the riddle, and Hugh Kenner has commented on the relationship of the kenning, a form of the riddle, to the ideogram (he does not, however, distinguish kenning and *kent heiti*): "Pound, it may be recalled, discovered Chinese after translating Anglo-Saxon. The Anglo-Saxon scholar's term for just such a vivid figure is 'kenning': the particulars by which the person or object in question is *known*. 'Whale-road,' 'soul-bearer,' are both ideogram and metaphor" (*The Poetry of Ezra Pound*, p. 89). The emblem can be seen as a metaphor existing in a dual medium; at the same time, the emblem method is the special use of metaphor that brings together a concrete image and an abstract concept.[8] The Image, a juxtaposition of elements without explicit connections, is a metaphor stripped of (or more often lying beneath) interpretive grammatical links.

When we consider language only, we see from the metaphor, the riddle, the emblem, and the ideogram (the ideogram of poetics, that is) that the skeletal form of all structures of phanopoeia is just this simple juxtaposition of elements:

candle/man

But simple juxtaposition does not remain simple. Parts of the juxtaposition will fit, giving us the "picture" in a riddle, and parts will not fit, giving us the "puzzle." We came to see that the "non-fit" is as essential as the "fit"; from both, spaces for fuller knowing are created. At a price, a selected dimension of these spaces can be made explicit and definite, laid out as a simile or in discursive prose explaining how, in the world of common sense, a man is in some respects like a candle. In any form, however, we seek to validate these juxtapositions by referring them back to the world of experience. Thus not just any juxtaposition will do. If a metaphor, then we ask for the significant metaphor, one which engenders thought, as Aristotle said, by teaching us to see something about the worlds of nature and of ourselves.

Aristotle's comments on metaphor in the *Poetics* and the *Rhetoric* make these connections between metaphor as a structure of language and metaphor as something that teaches us to see. He describes four structures of metaphor, the first three of which are what we now call synecdoche and metonymy. The fourth form, which is the fullest, most complex (and therefore to Aristotle the most pleasing) form of metaphor, is that built on a structure of natural proportion, $a:b::c:d$.[9] The riddles, emblems, and Images that juxtapose "candle" and "man" derive from seeing the proportional relationship:

$$\text{candle:flame: :man:life}$$

A test metaphor which for some reason is a favorite among literary critics is "the ship plows the waves." In Aristotle's terms, it is an expression of the proportion:

$$\text{ship:waves: :plow:earth}$$

We can doodle with this structure. Substituting terms according to the laws governing proportional relationships merely opens the metaphor out to the analogies, earth: waves: :plow:ship, or ship:plow: :waves:earth. But another law of proportions is that the product of the means equals the product of the extremes. Applying this to our proportional relationship (and silently passing over the question of just what exactly a word-product is), we have:

$$\text{earth-ship} = \text{waves-plow}$$

The operation, of questionable rigor, has turned up a kenning for "plow" ("earth-ship") and another for "ship" ("waves-plow"). ("What plows and plows, but no furrow remains?" asks a Danish riddle for "ship"—*ER*, p. 79.) The same operation performed on the proportion, candle: flame::man:life, gives us "candle's life" for "flame" and "man's flame" for "life," already conventional kennings in our language.

Sailing onward while the wind holds, we may try this operation on a more complex example:

> Dost thou not see my baby at my breast
> That sucks the nurse asleep?

The basic proportion takes the form, baby:nurse::asp: Cleopatra, and the operation performed above gives:

$$\text{Cleopatra-baby} = \text{asp-nurse}$$

It is not difficult to see "Cleopatra's baby" as a kenning (or riddle) for "asp," and "asp-nurse" as a kenning for "Cleopatra." Moreover, though they first fall out as kennings, the same structures may just as easily be seen as root forms of Images, ideograms, or, in the case of the relatively abstract "life," emblems—all forms of the basic power of phanopoeia.

Our manipulations with language have held up to this point, but in each case there is something left over. "That sucks the nurse asleep" shows that there is an action involved in this relationship, one that does not figure in the schematic proportion if we think of it only as a static relationship of four "things." A commentary on Aristotle's view of metaphor by Louis Mackey points this out again with respect to another Shakespearean example:

In the simile,
> As flies to wanton boys, are we to the gods;
> They kill us for their sport,

the grammatical form seems to state a logical "basis of comparison." But this basis—"They kill us for their sport"—does not *define* the analogy, flies:boys: :we: gods. Rather, it *complicates* it, and this is the power and the appeal of the simile: the relationship of flies to wanton boys receives an ominous theological qualification, and the relationship of man to God is debased by the suggestion of puerile caprice.[10]

The complication of "They kill us for their sport," which seems in some way to be even more basic to the metaphor than the concrete nouns set in proportion, is moreover an action, or as Fenollosa would say, "things in motion, motion in things." Aristotle's proportional relationship is not simply a grouping of quantities or "things," but a schematic expression of active relationships that have been seen. And what, after all, does our "equals" sign mean in our own operations above? "Earth-ship" does not *equal* "waves-plow," but certain equivalencies can be seen in the actions of plowing and sailing.[11] "Candle's life" does not equal "man's flame"; it is in the actions, burning and living, that we see important overlaps. And even in the actions there is not complete equality, but "non-fit" as well as "fit." The "block element" of the Danish riddle, "but no furrow remains," explicitly opens a space for the differences as well as the similarities between plowing and sailing. In the simile from *King Lear*, the "ominous theological qualification" and the "suggestion of puerile caprice" occupy these spaces. In Cleopatra's metaphor, "Cleopatra's baby" does not equal "asp-nurse," but the partial overlapping of the actions directs our eye to surprising equivalencies in life-giving and death-giving while maintaining the wide and fundamental differences between the two actions. It is necessary to see in Aristotle's proportion, then, a structure containing actions.

All this of course is exactly Fenollosa's view of metaphor and of the ideogram. He saw in metaphor a structure containing actions, and the Chinese ideogram as a visual representation of that structure. The ideogram, like the Image, is not a picture, not a snapshot. "The untruth of a painting or a photograph," he wrote, "is that, in spite of its concreteness, it drops the element of natural succession" (*CWC*, p. 9). As we have traced it, phanopoeia is a complex of three related powers: the visual power, the power of active intellectual patterning, and the power of catching up time and action in spatial form. Fenollosa's perspective on metaphor, from which "things are only the terminal points, or rather the meeting points, of actions," brings out this third power of phanopoeia, the circumscribing spatial pattern. Naming—not simply "names" but the act of naming—is a structuring of language that must include the active processes that have been seen and known. Time and action are caught in space, but looked at more closely, from within the form, simultaneous spatial pattern is seen as temporal progression. (There is nothing new about this: Boethius, and thus Dante and Chaucer, understood it perfectly some time ago.) It is therefore characteristic of phanopoeia that it does not bring us to a conclusion but circles us back to another beginning.

VI. CHARM

WE BEGIN again by turning to melopoeia and to the root forms of the music of lyric as they are heard in primitive literatures. We might first recall how Pound and Valéry described their struggles to find language for poems. Pound told us that the initiating impulse of his best-known Image poem was a moment of complex perception, the "sudden emotion" of seeing a pattern of beautiful faces in a metro station. The language he found for the poem presents that sudden emotion through the vision of the faces and petals on a wet, black bough seen together. It is a language of pattern, language organized by the power of phanopoeia, or, as Pound would say, language which seems as if sculpture or painting were just forced or forcing itself into words. It is, in short, a language of the visual imagination. Valéry, on the other hand, experienced a complex of rhythms set up in his mind's ear by a walk through Paris. The mental rhythms were based in a physical action, though Valéry also speaks of them as a "grace" descended upon his head. On that occasion the rhythms were too purely musical to go into poetry, but the experience allowed him to see that such rhythms often did initiate the processes of poetic composition for him. We can see how the language of such poetry would be language strongly organized by the power of melopoeia, language which seems to be music just forcing itself into articulate speech. We also note here, for future reflection, that Valéry called the rhythms a "magic," and he spoke of their bringing a "sense of strangeness" he found almost unbearable.

Valéry's observations of the initiating processes of poetry in his own mind suggest that the sources of the melopoeia of poetry lie in the music of pure, physical rhythm. Northrop Frye, however, has suggested another source for the music of lyric poetry in particular. The distinctive music of lyric, he feels, grows out of language itself. It begins in a subconscious babbling among the sounds of words, and out of the associative possibilities in the sounds of words arises a controlling rhythm—"an oracular, meditative, irregular, unpredictable, and essentially discontinuous rhythm, emerging from the coincidences of the sound-pattern" (*Anatomy of Criticism*, p. 271). Along its musical axis, then, the language of lyric is primarily organized by an irregular rhythm of sound-echoes, and this rhythm is the primary rhythm of lyric even when it is used in combination with a continuous metrical pattern or the rhetorical rhythms of speech. A major concern of modern lyric poetry, Frye notes, has been to liberate this distinctive rhythm: "The aim of 'free' verse is not simply revolt against metre and *epos* conventions, but the articulation of an independent rhythm equally distinct from metre and from prose. If we do not recognize this third rhythm, we shall have no answer for the naive objection that when poetry loses regular metre it becomes prose" (p. 272). We have already seen that Frye identifies the radical form of this distinctive music (or *melos*) as *charm*.

Valéry, then, heard the musical roots of poetry in the wordless rhythms of music itself. Frye suggests that the musical roots of lyric lie instead in the irregular rhythms growing out of the sounds of words. Pound, when he described melopoeia as poetry "wherein the words are charged, over and above their plain meaning, with some musical property, which directs the bearing or trend of that meaning," did not speculate on the sources of those musical properties. He did, however, distinguish three kinds of melopoeia: " (1) that made to be sung to a tune; (2) that made to be intoned or sung to a sort of chant; and (3) that made to be spoken; and the art of joining words in each of these kinds is different, and cannot be clearly understood until the reader knows that there are three different objectives."[1] Since the objective of each form of melopoeia is different, Pound says, the art of organizing language in each form is different. One form aims at song, one at a kind of chant-verse, and the third seems to aim at the goal of Words-worth's poet, "a selection of the language really spoken by men," or poetry primarily organized by the rhythms of speech.

Gathering these suggestions together, we will begin our discussion with the assumption that there are three roots of the melopoeia of lyric poetry: (1) *song*, words sung to the rhythm and melody of music; (2) *charm*, magic incantation carried on the singsong voice of a magician at work; (3) *speech*, the music we probably are most accustomed to hear-ing in poetry, and in good prose as well. (Pound's "chant-verse," I believe, is not a radical form, though close to one; this is discussed in the following chapter.) As powers that organize the language of lyric, the three forms of melopoeia will be referred to as song-melos, charm-melos, and speech-melos. The first two derive from the roots of song and charm in the language of poetry. The third derives from the music of the spoken language, which is a root as well, and poets will say that it is the only source of their lan-guage when they think their audience can no longer hear the buried music of the first two roots.

In Aristotle, μέλος means song, and also the music to which the words of a song are set. This, like the word "lyric" itself —originally referring to the poet's lyre—would seem to direct our search for the roots of this power back to the union of poetry and song, and especially to primitive cul-tures, in which poetry is seldom found separate from music and song. But along with the Greek word there is the Latin word *carmen*, attracting English critics from Sidney on-wards by its closeness to the word "charm." It is more than coincidence: *carmen* generally means song or poem, but in older Latin texts it also means a magic formula, an incan-tation. Here is another root of lyric melopoeia, and it does

seem to be a way of organizing language that is distinct
from the way of song. When we go back to primitive literatures we find that song and charm are two different things.
First of all, they aim at different effects: in primitive societies songs can be sung simply for pleasure, but charms
are intended to perform a quite different function. Also,
songs are open to the society, meant for everyone, but
charms are closed, secret, and hidden. The vocabulary of
the songs is drawn from the ordinary spoken language of
the society, but the words of a charm are likely to involve
a special language. Most importantly, the rhythms of the
two forms differ, along the lines of our distinctions. Songs
are organized by the external rhythms of music, and in
primitive societies this usually includes the rhythms of dancing, drumming, and even acting. The rhythm of charms,
on the other hand, grows out of the internal rhythms of the
words themselves. We heard both rhythms recalled in
Blake's "Tyger," the song-rhythm of nursery rhymes and
game-songs, and the charm-rhythm developed by the assonances, alliterations, rhymes, and word-repetitions in the
language of the poem.

Like other kinds of rhythm, the irregular rhythm of the
words in a charm is a function of repetition—"coincidences
of the sound-pattern." Repetition is an essentially musical
procedure, and in poetry it is the basic structural principle
of melopoeia. It stands in the same relation to melopoeia
as spatial juxtaposition does to phanopoeia. The skeletal
form of the riddles, emblems, Images, ideograms, and metaphors of phanopoeia, we saw, is a simple juxtaposition of
two or more elements: candle/man. It is a spatial structure
of the visual imagination, as repetition is a temporal structure of what we have called the aural imagination. Valéry
sensed a common ground somewhere beneath both structures, and, as the ideogram shows, transformations are possible. With the ideogram, spatial form can be seen as a
transformation of temporal form, and temporal form as a
transformation of spatial form. Phrases such as "the rhythm

of images" or "the pattern of rhythms" are slippery but useful attempts by critics to deal with these transformations, and "the coincidences of the sound-pattern" is another such phrase. The idea of rhythmical pattern has interesting implications in the charms, but we will defer these until we have listened to some of the actual sound-patterns of charms and have seen how they are intended to work.

The repetition of sounds in the language, and the rhythms that grow out of the recurring sounds, are striking and consistent characteristics of the melopoeia of primitive charms. Although such rhythms are heard throughout primitive poetry in general, and are the source of what is often called its incantatory quality, they seem to organize and to dominate charm-language most of all and are heard at their strongest there, as in the repetitions of words and of apparently meaningless syllables in an Eskimo charm for good weather:

> nuyuamingi nuyuamingi
> nuyuamingi nuyuaming atang ai yanga
> ye yi ya ye yi yanga yanga yanga
> nuyuamingi nuyuamingi
> nuyuamingi nuyuaming atang ai yang

> Clouds, clouds,
> Clouds, clouds down below,
> Clouds, clouds,
> Clouds, clouds down below.[2]

Many primitive charms simply repeat a few words or a single line over and over as often as is necessary for the charm to work its effect. Such is the following children's charm from the aborigines of South Australia. It consists of four words which set up, through their interlocking sound-repetitions, the necessary incantatory pattern to charm a falling star—to the children an evil spirit—back to where it belongs:

Kandanga daruarungu manangga gilbanga

star: falling: at night time: you [star] go back.[3]

We might think of Blake's "Tyger" again, and hear in it
now a similar exorcism, a frightened child's voice trying to
charm away the bright terror in the forests of the night. The
rhythms of charming, in both the Australian charm and the
Blake poem, are carried by thick coincidences of the sound-
pattern, insistently repeated vowel and consonant sounds.

In looking at transcriptions of primitive texts, however,
we must be cautious against generalizing too much about the
use of sound in primitive poetry, for this requires a trained
field worker's knowledge of the native language. Although
many primitive texts appear to make conscious use of rhyme,
for example, the anthropologist John Greenway has stated
that conscious rhyme is almost never found in primitive
literature: "Where rhyme occurs among preliterate peoples,
it appears to be either a contribution of the recorder . . .
or is induced by the form of the language. Polynesians in-
sulated one consonant from another with vowels, which
produced what some scholars think is deliberate rhyme."
Greenway gives as an example a Hawaiian mythological
song, ostensibly a rhyming poem. "But," he goes on, "there
are two things that disqualify this as rhyme: first, when
properly pronounced, only two of the couplets rhyme; second, all the other words in the song end in vowels, and if
these words were arranged in random fashion, they would
rhyme as well as in the meaningful syntax. Some Australian
languages produce this automatic rhyme also; the Aranda
tongue ends nearly all its words with '-a,' so that an Aranda
song can hardly avoid rhyme."[4]

The warning is necessary, but Greenway's mention of the
"automatic rhyme" in some native languages will set the
serious student of babble to further speculations. It is an old-
fashioned and discredited procedure to draw parallels between the early development of language in children and

the structures of fully developed languages, primitive or otherwise, which have a long history behind them. Yet it is still interesting to note how a child's babbling of repeated sounds (*mama, papa, bowwow*) leads, with the encouraging reactions of mama and papa and perhaps bowwow, to meaningful words, and then to notice the large number of words in certain languages that appear to be formed on the same pattern. A glance at texts in the Melanesian languages of the southwestern Pacific islands turns up words in Dobuan such as *lulu* ("to sing"), *kenokeno* ("to lie down"), *bwegabwegai* ("to shed, to break out of"), *ladiladi* ("sweet sounding"), and *bwebweso* (the home of the dead). In the Trobriand Islands, natives talk about their yam-gardens using everyday words such as *pwaypwaya* ("earth, soil for planting"), *munumunu* ("weed"), *lala* ("to flower"), *puripuri* ("the bursting forth of fruits"), *bwabwa'u* ("black," the color of ripe yams), *ginigini* ("to carve"), and *ula'ula* ("first-fruit offerings"). Some of these words, moreover, are conscious reduplicative forms, words formed by syllable-doubling or word-doubling such as that used in Greek for the formation of the perfect aspect of verbs, in other languages to indicate plurality in nouns or the superlative degree of adjectives, and in Dobuan to signify temporal continuity.[5] The suggestion is that sound-repetition is a vital root in the development of language itself. Greenway is concerned about whether or not rhyme is present in primitive texts as a conscious artistic element; we can wonder if in some cases the echoing babble of sound-repetitions took place not at the formation of the individual charm but at the formation of the language. It is melopoeia's counterpart to Fenollosa's theory that the roots of poetry lie in the structures of language.

The coincidences of the sound-pattern are there in primitive charms, though it is not clear why they are there. If full end-rhyme is rare, the internal soundings of consonance, assonance, alliteration, and word-repetition are common. To take a few more examples, we can hear some of these patterns in an Eskimo charm collected by Knud Rasmussen:

Magic words to be said in the morning when rising.

> nuna-maso
> nunarshuaq-maso
> uwsha makua
> taiklap inukshua
> silarshop avershue
> patqarai
> qakerai.

> Land earth-root
> Great land earth-root
> Here is these
> Song-texts' master
> The world's pillars
> They pale,
> They turn white.[6]

The transcription of the native text is a rough approximation, but it is worth trying aloud. To learn about rhythm and rhyme, Pound wrote, "Let the candidate fill his mind with the finest cadences he can discover, preferably in a foreign language, so that the meaning of the words may be less likely to divert his attention from the movement; e.g. Saxon charms, Hebridean Folk Songs, the verse of Dante, and the lyrics of Shakespeare—if he can dissociate the vocabulary from the cadence" (*Literary Essays*, p. 5).

A long fertility charm collected by Bronislaw Malinowski in the Trobriand Islands illustrates many of the rhythms of sound-associations, both in the irregular echoing of vowels and consonants and in the more regular repetition of words and phrases. This charm is the central element of a magic ritual that inaugurates a new planting season with the clearing of the land for the next year's yam-gardens. It opens with a blessing-word which Malinowski says is "especially directed towards the depth of the earth; it also implies firmness and permanence of the crops and conveys

the idea of going down and rising again." It is delivered
in the melodious singsong characteristic of charms:

> Vatuvi, vatuvi,
> Vatuvi, vatuvi,
> Vitumaga, i-maga.
> Vatuvi, vatuvi,
> Vatuvi, vatuvi,
> Vitulola, i-lola.

Show the way, show the way,
Show the way, show the way,
Show the way groundwards, into the deep ground.
Show the way, show the way,
Show the way, show the way,
Show the way firmly, show the way to the firm moorings.

Next follows a series of names calling on ancestors, from
the more distant ancestral spirits down to the magician's
own grandfather and father:

> Tubu-gu Polu,
> tubu-gu Koleko,
> tubu-gu Takikila,
> tubu-gu Mulabwoyta,
> tubu-gu Kwayudila,
> tubu-gu Katupwala,
> tubu-gu Bugwabwaga,
> tubu-gu Purayasi,
> tubu-gu Numakala;
> bilumava'u biloma-m,
> tabu-gu Mwakenuwa,
> tama-gu Yowana.

O grandfathers of the name of Polu,
O grandfathers of the name of Koleko,
O grandfathers of the name of Takikila,
O grandfathers of the name of Mulabwoyta,

141

O grandfathers of the name of Kwayudila,
O grandfathers of the name of Katupwala,
O grandfathers of the name of Bugwabwaga,
O grandfathers of the name of Purayasi,
O grandfathers of the name of Numakala;
and thou, new spirit,
my grandfather Mwakenuwa,
and thou my father Yowana.

The next section is directed at the land that will be culti-
vated, and that, the charm says, will be fertile and swell
with ripe yams:

I-gebile lopou-la ulo buyagu;
i-tokaye lopou-la ulo buyagu;
i-takubila lopou-la ulo buyagu;
i-gibage'u lopou-la ulo buyagu;
i-kabwabu lopou-la ulo buyagu;
i-gibukwayu'u lopou-la ulo buyagu;
i-gibakayaulo lopou-la ulo buyagu;
i-tawaga lopou-la ulo buyagu;
i-kabina'i lopou-la ulo buyagu;
i-kabinaygwadi lopou-la ulo buyagu;
a-tabe'u!

The belly of my garden leavens,
The belly of my garden rises,
The belly of my garden reclines,
The belly of my garden grows to the size of a bush-hen's
    nest,
The belly of my garden grows like an ant-hill;
The belly of my garden rises and is bowed down,
The belly of my garden rises like the iron-wood palm,
The belly of my garden lies down,
The belly of my garden swells,
The belly of my garden swells as with a child.
I sweep away!

142

The charm continues with a long list of pests and blights which are swept away, blown away, driven away—exorcised from the yam-garden (*Coral Gardens and Their Magic*, I, 96-98; II, 255-65).

The rhythms of garden-magic are not foreign to English poetry, and an example of these rhythms can be heard in a charm familiar to students of English literature. The Old English charm for unfruitful land, or land under an evil spell, sets up a strong incantatory rhythm through sound-patterns of repeated words, alliteration, assonance, and homoeoteleuton:

> Erce, Erce, Erce,   eorþan modor,
> geunne þe se alwalda,   ece drihten,
> æcera wexendra   and wridendra,
> eacniendra   and elniendra,
> sceafta hehra,   scirra wæstma,
> and þæra bradan   berewæstma,
> and þæra hwitan   hwætewæstma,
> and ealra   eorþan wæstma.[7]

> Erce, Erce, Erce, mother of land,
> may the all-ruler, the eternal lord, grant you
> fields growing and flourishing,
> increasing and growing strong,
> shafts of high blades, bright harvests,
> and the broad barley-harvests,
> and the white wheat-harvests,
> and all the harvests of the land.

This is a fairly "late" version of a charm, and the rhythm is almost too strong here. Although the rhythm is not what any Old English scholar would call regular, the sound-patterns of the words have been influenced by the traditional versification of Old English *epos*, and the charm itself has received an overlay of Christian prayer. Beneath these, however, the Old English charms, far more than the Old

English riddles, still retain their older and deeper roots, and still carry the strange, irregular music of the language of primitive charms.

Behind incantation stands enchantment. The basis of any charm is something that we might neglect but that its original users would never forget, its magic. Charms are meant to make things happen, to cause action. There is no "chance" in primitive cosmologies, anthropologists tell us: wind and rain, fertility of the land, success in trading, human love, sickness and healing, or the arrival of death are always *caused*, by something or (more often) by someone. Charm magic tries to control these events by manipulation of the hidden forces in nature. The Trobriand garden-charm encourages yam-growth and drives away pests and blights; the Old English charm for infertile land, in addition to the growth-producing section given above, goes on to ward off malignant spells of witchcraft or sorcery. To exercise these powers, every charm uses more than just words. By basic laws of magic, a charm must also use an action to get an action. The action may simply consist of facing in the right direction while the charm is being said, or it may be an elaborate ritual connected in some "sympathetic" or "contagious" way with the purpose of the charm.

The English charm must be accompanied by an involved set of primitive rituals and Christian prayers to be effective. For plowed land, the magic action requires unknown seed taken from beggars (who are given a double portion in return), incense, fennel, holy soap, and holy salt to be placed in a hole bored in the beam of the plow. The charm is spoken over the plow, and the first furrow is made. Under this first furrow is then laid a loaf made of meal of every kind and kneaded with milk and holy water. When the Trobriand charm is first used in the seasonal cycle of garden-magic, it is spoken by the magician over the axes that will be used for clearing the land on the next morning. The axes lie on mats in his hut, and on each axe is a mixture of magic herbs the magician has collected. Over the axes another mat is laid, forming what Malinowski calls a "voice-trap" into which the charm is then spoken. Finally a banana leaf is wrapped and tied around the cutting edge of each axe blade to enclose the magic herbs and the spell-carrying breath of the magician, powers that will be carried to the garden site in the morning.

This sort of thing may seem to take us somewhat afield from the language of lyric poetry, yet the magic actions of a charm are a necessary component of the whole and cannot be neglected. The point is that charms are first and foremost concerned with power, with the use of magic words and magic actions to cause crops to grow, game to come, or another's spells to be defeated. And since the magic of a charm is its basic purpose, this purpose influences the language of charms, the structures of the words. In certain ways, I believe, it must even be a source of these structures. It is the sense of sacred formality, the *necessity* for the compelling, incantatory quality, that produces the rich webs of sound in charms. At the roots, the words of a charm are themselves magic actions. Aldous Huxley recognized this when he argued that magic spells have to be poetry and the magicians who make them poets: "The thing is psychologically inevitable. If words had not first moved him, how could man have come to believe that they would move things? And is it likely that he would set out to move things by means of incantations which left him unmoved? But words which move are poetry. Magicians, I repeat, are always poets."[8]

Two widely separated examples may suggest this important sense of words which move. The irregular rhythms of sound-associations are evident in both charms, but we can hear them now as part of the larger context of magical power. A magician-poet among the Semang of the Malay

Peninsula made a short love-charm intended to pull the beloved irresistibly to the lover. For the ritual action to be performed, a small, rare plant called chinduai must first be found. It is pulled up, a little oil is dropped on it, and then oil from the plant is smeared on the lover's forehead and breast. Then the charm is spoken:

> En-en Bonn,
> Ta-ta' noi,
> Nai ka-bleb,
> Chuang boi,
> Chepöi döoi
> Tug-tug loi.

> Look, look, comrade!
> As this oil drips,
> Alone by yourself
> Approach towards me,
> [And] yearn towards me
> [As this] oil spreads upwards.[9]

The magic controls both the application of the oil and the incantation, the ritual action and the words of this charm, bending them to the right shape for sending forth their power.

A very different charm is a Cherokee formula for killing an enemy. The curse is a form of charm that lies behind the literary forms of invective, flyting, and satire.[10] But if the literary forms have become "just words," the magic of a curse proposes much more. The ritual action of this Cherokee charm begins with the sorcerer secretly obtaining some of the victim's spittle. He puts it into a tube with a joint of a poisonous plant, seven earthworms beaten into a paste, and splinters from a tree that has been struck by lightning. The tube is then buried in the forest at the base of a tree, again one that has been struck and infused with the power of lightning:

Didálatlí'ti

Sge!

Nágwa tsudantági tegúyatawáilatelíga.

Iyusti (————) tsilastú'li.

Iyústi (————) ditsadáita.

Tsuwatsíla elawíni tsidáhistaníga.

Tsudantagi elawíni tsidáhistaníga.

Núya gúnage guyútlutaníga.

A'nuwági gúnagé guyútlutaníga.

Sutalúga gúnage degúyanúgalútaníga, tsúnanugáisti
    nigésuna.

Usuhíyi nunáhi witétsatanúusi gunésa gúnage asahalagí.

Tsutúnelíga.

Elawáti asáhalagí áduníga.

Usinulíyu Usuhíyi gultsáte digúnagestáyi, elawáti
    gúnage tidáhisti wa'yanúgalutsíga.

Gunésa gúnage sutalúga gúnage gayútlutaníga.

Tsudantági uskálutsíga.

Sa'káni aduníga.

Usúhita atanísséti, ayálatsísesti tsudantági, tsúnanugáisti
    nigésuna.

Sge!

To Destroy Life

Listen!

Now I have come to step over your soul.

You are of the (wolf) clan.

Your name is (A'yúini).

Your spittle I have put at rest under the earth.

Your soul I have put at rest under the earth.

I have come to cover you over with the black rock.

I have come to cover you over with the black cloth.

I have come to cover you with the black slabs, never
    to reappear.

Toward the black coffin of the upland in the Darkening
    Land your paths shall stretch out.

So shall it be for you.
The clay of the upland has come [to cover you. (?)]
Instantly the black clay has lodged there where it is at
   rest at the black houses in the Darkening Land.
With the black coffin and with the black slabs I have
   come to cover you.
Now your soul has faded away.
It has become blue.
When darkness comes your spirit shall grow less and
   dwindle away, never to reappear.
Listen![11]

(The blanks in the opening lines are for the name and clan
of the victim.) Like other Indian tribes, the Cherokees have
a color symbolism associated with the cardinal directions.
Black is associated with the west and signifies death—it is
naturally the dominant color in this charm. Blue is associated with the north and signifies defeat or trouble, and
it is often used in their charms to mean an uneasiness of
mind, a sorrow, or disappointment. When, near the end,
this charm says that the victim's soul "has become blue,"
it indicates that his soul is already beginning to be aware
of the effects of the charm, is already feeling in itself the
weakening and the shrinking that will continue until it
dwindles away ("The Sacred Formulas of the Cherokees,"
pp. 242, 390-92). A look at the Cherokee text reveals that
the repetitions of sound and of word are there—some of
them, perhaps, induced by the form of the language, but
they are nevertheless there. I think that it is much more
likely they are there because the magic requires that they
be there. In order to get the power to kill an enemy, the
Cherokee sorcerer had to find words which move, and in
doing so found the strange beauty of this charm.

Even when it leaves the world of primitive magic, poetry
will often retain that archaic sense of casting a spell, of
magical compulsion, that comes to it from charm. If
they recognize it, poets tend to respect this old voice when

they come upon it, even in the face of much more reasonable demands made by the poem. Poe is famous for valuing this sense, even for forcing it, and his famous lines from "The City in the Sea," with their rich coincidences of sound, are a good charm:

> Whose wreathéd friezes intertwine
> The viol, the violet, and the vine.

Some readers, however, have not been moved. The first edition of the poem had exotic "Babylon-like" walls,

> Whose entablatures intertwine
> The mask—the viol—and the vine,

a version that Poe dropped when the incantatory voice surfaced. Paul Fussell, among other good critics, prefers the clearer sense of the first version: "But for Poe music must take precedence over even symbolism and semantic meaning, and he revises the passage until it stands as the very locus classicus of sweetness overtaking sense." Roy Harvey Pearce has taken a similar critical stance against certain poems of William Carlos Williams, poems in which, he complains, "the incantatory overrides logic, structure, and the disposition of meaning."[12]

The appearance of that archaic voice in poetry is difficult to describe and impossible to defend against demands for "sense." Paul Valéry, ever concerned with the rhythms of melopoeia, was convinced of its importance, yet his statements can hardly be called arguments:

> It must not be forgotten that for centuries poetry was used for purposes of enchantment. Those who took part in these strange operations had to believe in the power of the word, and far more in the efficacy of its sound than in its significance. Magic formulas are often without meaning; but it was never thought that their power depended on their intellectual content.

Let us listen to lines like these:

Mère des souvenirs, maîtresse des maîtresses . . .

or

Sois sage, ô ma Douleur, et tiens-toi plus tranquille. . . .

These words work on us (or at least on some of us) without telling us very much. They tell us, perhaps, that they have nothing to tell us; that, by the very means which usually tell us something, they are exercising a quite different function.

(The Art of Poetry, pp. 74-75)

In charms, Valéry understood, the power of the words lies far more in their sounds than in their literal significance. It is a language of deep roots. The ethnologists who collect primitive charms face a particularly difficult problem when they try to determine the meaning, the "sense" made by the words in a charm. In collecting Eskimo charms, Diamond Jenness and Knud Rasmussen both noted striking differences between the language of the charms and the language of ordinary speech, and Rasmussen suggested that the charms employed a special language of the shamans, sometimes with ancient words that had fallen into disuse. W. W. Skeat, son of the great philologist, said that he spent many hours trying to discover the exact meaning of the Semang love-charm; the language was not the ordinary Semang dialect but belonged, he felt, to a more archaic dialect. James Mooney also believed that the special language of the Cherokee charms he had uncovered was archaic and came from the nearly extinct Eastern, or "Lower Cherokee," dialect, and a later collector thought that, in addition to a level of archaic words, there were influences from the Western, or "Upper Cherokee," dialect. (The ordinary spoken language of the tribe is the Central, or "Middle Cherokee," dialect.) R. F. Fortune, reporting on Dobuan charms, pointed out simply, "The words of Dobuan magic are not words of ordinary speech. They form a secret esoteric language, a language of power." Bronislaw

Malinowski discussed at length the special languge of the Trobriand charms. One example is the word *vatuvi*, the key word opening the garden-charm above, and a form never found in ordinary speech.[13] Old English scholars have been similarly troubled by the meanings of the word *Erce* which opens the charm for infertile land, and they usually gloss it either as the lost name of a Germanic fertility goddess or else as "meaningless incantation."

The language of the charms is not entirely, or even nearly all, a special language, but it does contain many mysterious elements which ethnologists trace to special "magic names" for things, to words that may be from distant or archaic dialects, to obscure mythological references or topographical allusions, and to strange usages of syntax, morphology, and phonology. Native informants have their own explanations of this language, and when pressed by an ethnologist for exact translations they will usually slide by, as the Cherokees do, by saying that "this was the way it was said by the people who lived a long time ago" (*The Swimmer Manuscript*, p. 163). The charms, as they know, are fixed, traditional texts that have been handed down from a long time ago through a line of trained magicians, the ultimate source being, perhaps, a mythological power or culture hero. Magic words are believed by the Trobriand Islanders to be something that came into existence at the very beginning of things, coeval with the other powers of the world, and that is why they work on those powers. Magic language is primeval language, and naturally it is different from the language of ordinary speech; it is "true speech," distinct from "the way of talk" (*Coral Gardens and Their Magic*, II, 216-18, 222-23).

To produce an effect, the charms must use, along with ritual actions, words capable of acting, words felt to be themselves actions, and something important is missed if we explain these obscure and mysterious elements of "true speech" as survivals of archaic dialects or as simply "meaningless incantation." Although both explanations are in many cases true, their truth does not go deep enough. The language that has been selected for magic use, a language of strange, irregular rhythms and rich nets of sound-pattern, was felt to be, as R. F. Fortune said, a special language of power. Malinowski called this element in charm language the "coefficient of weirdness":

> If the main principle of magical belief is that words exercise power in virtue of their primeval mysterious connexion with some aspect of reality, then obviously we must not expect the words of Trobriand magic to act in virtue of their ordinary colloquial meaning. A spell is believed to be a primeval text which somehow came into being side by side with animals and plants, with winds and waves, with human disease, human courage and human frailty. Why should such words be as the words of common speech? They are not uttered to carry ordinary information from man to man, or to give advice or an order. The natives might naturally expect all such words to be very mysterious and far removed from ordinary speech. And so they are to a large extent, but by no means completely.

Much of the vocabulary, grammar, and prosody of the language of the charms, he goes on to say, "falls into line with the deeply ingrained belief that magical speech must be cast in another mould, because it is derived from other sources and produces different effects from ordinary speech" (*Coral Gardens and Their Magic*, II, 218). *Vatuvi*, for example, in form neither noun nor verb, is a special inaugurative word "launched freely into the substances to be charmed, the herbs, the axes, the torches and digging-sticks. It has got no context of direct connexion with any specific thing or agency. It has to be taken as a verbal missile of magical power—a conception very much in harmony with the repetitive character of its utterance, whereby it is rubbed into the substance" (II, 248). Another such verbal missile, we can believe, was the inaugurative Old English word *Erce,* directed into the mixture of seeds, incense, fennel, holy soap, and holy salt in the plow. It belonged to the language of magic power—meaningless to us, perhaps, but then it was not meant for us.

In the search for words which move, then, the language of magic sought out what became the melopoeia of charms, a special language of webs of sound and irregular rhythms different from the language used to communicate ordinary meanings. But it is not "meaningless" language—how could it be? The language is different from ordinary speech because, as Malinowski says, it is derived from other sources and produces different effects. Nor is it simply a question of archaic vocabulary and syntax, the sort of thing we would call poetic diction. The special language of the charms represents a much deeper encroachment of melopoeia into the area of logopoeia or *lexis;* it is derived not from old meanings but from old powers of sound and rhythm flowing into and shaping the language—a difference not of diction but of basic structure. The language of the charms is a language of power, and that power comes primarily not from lexical meanings, archaic or colloquial, but from other meanings hidden deep in the sounds and rhythms.

But here we must pause to protect our flank, for when the charm radical appears too openly in the language poets use, in Poe's language for example, literary critics can become very skeptical. To suggest that incantatory sound and rhythm are in some cases *meant* to override the logical meanings in a lyric poem is in some quarters asking for trouble. We are nevertheless not in any essential disagreement with critics such as I. A. Richards, John Crowe Ransom, or W. K. Wimsatt, who are concerned with the complexities of semantic and analogical meanings in a poem, who feel that sound and rhythm are important only as they contribute to and complicate these prior meanings, and who, moreover, are devastatingly adept at demonstrating how a similar sound-pattern has quite different effects when it is placed in different semantic contexts—thus proving that sound-patterns have no "poetic" functions on their own. There is no disagreement so long as it is recognized that these demonstrations are not talking about roots. Their method begins with the finished product, the meanings a poem has developed through word and image, and then works backward to the sound-patterns of the poem. When it gets down to sound and rhythm, it is concerned not with melopoeia but with a kind of onomatopoeia, an imitation in sound of lexical meaning. It is a method that is oriented toward phanopoeia, and it considers (and ultimately disqualifies) sound as a possible element in the juxtaposition of two meanings.[14] Melopoeia by itself can make no claim for clear lexical meaning. If, as Eliot suggested, "genuine poetry can communicate before it is understood," clearly what such poetry communicates before it is understood is not an understandable meaning. The rhythm of the charm root exercises, in Valéry's words, a quite different function.

As he often does, Pound gives the impression of having thought about and settled all this for himself some time ago. Discussing phanopoeia and melopoeia as they affect both prose and poetry, he wrote:

In *Phanopoeia* we find the greatest drive toward utter precision of word; this art [prose] exists almost exclusively by it.

In *melopoeia* we find a contrary current, a force tending often to lull, or to distract the reader from the exact sense of the language. It is poetry on the borders of music and music is perhaps the bridge between consciousness and the unthinking sentient or even insentient universe. (*Literary Essays*, p. 26)

Both ways of charging language are of course sources of good poetry. Phanopoeia in poetry drives toward precision of image and thought, the clear, precise seeing and knowing that is needed for a good riddle or a good Image poem.

Melopoeia, on the other hand, is a force that leads poetry away from precisions of word and meaning, but that may be, as Pound said, a bridge to a non-verbal consciousness. The words of a charm are not derived from seeing and knowing but from the actions of the sound-patterns, and they are concerned not with vision but with power.

The primary interest of the charm for us is as a subterranean root feeding the growth of more complex forms of lyric, but we also find, as we did with the riddles, that from time to time poets are attracted into conscious literary imitations of the primitive form. These are of interest to criticism because they give us a poet's view of an important root of his art, and, further, because with some poets even a conscious imitation manifests the power of the old roots. Shakespeare's imitation of a charm in *Macbeth* has been successful enough:

> *1 Witch.* Round about the cauldron go;
> In the poison'd entrails throw.
> Toad that under cold stone
> Days and nights has thirty-one
> Swelt'red venom sleeping got
> Boil thou first i' th' charmed pot.
> *All.* Double, double toil and trouble;
> Fire burn, and cauldron bubble.

The first part gives the directions for the magic actions, and the second part, with the thick, internal repetitions of sound, gives the magic words. Shakespeare probably had in mind the spells, found throughout the witchcraft-lore of the period, for invoking the powers of darkness, and in the play his charm imitates their effects as well as their words: the ritual actions are performed, the words are spoken, and Macbeth appears—drawn onto the scene for more dark equivocations that will spur his vaulting ambition.

For most people, however, Ariel's lovely charm in *The Tempest* casts more of a spell:

Full fathom five thy father lies;
    Of his bones are coral made;
Those are pearls that were his eyes;
    Nothing of him that doth fade
But doth suffer a sea-change
Into something rich and strange.
Sea-nymphs hourly ring his knell:
Burden.   Ding-dong.
    Hark! now I hear them—Ding-dong bell.

The witches' charm has the obvious rhythms of charm, but the sound-patterns in Ariel's charm—the assonances, alliterations, rhymes, and the subtle movements as one vowel-sound or consonant-sound changes to another—generate deeper, far more elusive rhythms and a magic that is truly something rich and strange. Productions of *The Tempest* usually set this charm to the music of Elizabethan song, adding an outside rhythm and melody to the words, but the words themselves have the irregular, internal rhythms of a much older music. And again it is as a charm that it works in the play: Ferdinand, close to despair over his father's apparent drowning, is drawn by this charm to Miranda, even though he does not understand its words of transformation and rebirth.

Pound also wrote a literary imitation of a charm, a "chant for the transmutation of metals" called "The Alchemist," which uses names hinting of old, mysterious, Greek and Romance origins to help generate the charmed sound-patterns. Two sections of it:

Saîl of Claustra, Aelis, Azalais,
As you move among the bright trees;
As your voices, under the larches of Paradise
Make a clear sound,
Saîl of Claustra, Aelis, Azalais,
Raimona, Tibors, Berangèrë,
'Neath the dark gleam of the sky;

Under night, the peacock-throated,
Bring the saffron-coloured shell,
Bring the red gold of the maple,
Bring the light of the birch tree in autumn
Mirals, Cembelins, Audiarda,
Remember this fire.

.   .   .   .

Midonz, with the gold of the sun, the leaf of the poplar,
by the light of the amber,
Midonz, daughter of the sun, shaft of the tree, silver of
the leaf, light of the yellow of the amber,
Midonz, gift of the God, gift of the light, gift of the
amber of the sun,
Give light to the metal.
(*Personae*, p. 75)

The poem shows, I believe, that Pound understood the charm. He understood the irregular rhythms generated by word-repetitions and rich vowel-patterns, and he understood the kind of magic that would be necessary to give light to the dark metal, to transform raw elements into gold or into poetry. The archaic music of charms surfaces again throughout *The Cantos*, and we hear it in the Tamuz-Adonis ritual of Canto XLVII, where fragments of old language from Bion's lament for Adonis become a charm for fertility and healing (Τυ Διῶνα, Και Μοῖραι / Και Μοῖραι' Ἀδονιν); in Canto LXXIX, where in the language of a European folk charm the lynx of Dionysos is called up by Pound as a protection-charm in the Pisan cage ("O Lynx keep watch on my fire"); and as late as the fragmentary rite of Canto CXII:

. . . owl, and wagtail
and huo³-hu², the fire-fox
Amṛta, that is nectar
white wind, white dew

Here from the beginning, we have been here
from the beginning
From her breath were the goddesses
²La²muɳ³mi
If we did not perform ²Ndaw ¹bpö
nothing is solid
without ²Mùaɳ ¹bpö
no reality. . . .

Except for the Sanskrit *Amṛta* ("the nectar conferring im-
mortality"), the special language here is the Tibeto-Burman
language of the Na-khi tribesmen of southwest China, and
it comes from a ceremony of purification and fertility. The
rest of the short Canto CXII adds two Chinese ideograms,
two Latin names for sacred plants used in the Na-khi ceremony, and two pictographs from the sacred texts of the
Na-khi.[15] The result is a literary charm that attempts to
recreate a special language and rite of power. Like the
charms of Trobriand garden-magic, Pound's charm calls on
the power of sounding words and the power of ritual actions
as realities which, like wind and dew, "have been here /
from the beginning."

Pound's literary charms recover a further element of
power in the charm radical, the magic of names. All three
charms from *The Cantos* use names as a source of sound
and of power, and the rich-sounding names in "The Alchemist" are all names of women, some thirty-five in all
in the complete poem, taken from the old literatures of
southern Europe. The magic of names is an old root in
poetry that derives from the charm and its concern with
power. Primitive cultures, and the anthropologists who
study them, must pay careful attention to the use or avoid-
ance of names by members of a society, and this general
feeling for the power, and the danger, of names appears
particularly in the language of the society's charms. In the
charms, naming can include the formal repetition of ordi-

nary names for things which are being approached in a non-ordinary way, the use of special "magic names" which hold power over things, and the calling of secret, holy names of powerful, though often vaguely realized, mythological figures or forces. The weather-charm from the Copper Eskimos depends on the repeated naming of the clouds for much of its power ("Clouds, clouds . . ."), as the Australian charm for a falling star drives away the evil spirit by naming it ("star: falling: at night time"). The charm-voice that emerges from one of the depths of "The Tyger" begins similarly with the naming of the bright terror ("Tyger Tyger, burning bright"). The section of the Trobriand garden-charm naming the long line of magician-ancestors both invokes their power and establishes their presence in the ceremony; "the list of ancestors affirms the magician's charter," Malinowski writes, "while at the same time the names of those who had so much to do with fertility in the past possess a fertilising influence" (*Coral Gardens and Their Magic*, II, 259). On the malefic side of the charms is the necessity of the name and the clan of the victim in the Cherokee curse "To Destroy Life."

The reality of names and the power residing in them often persists into literate cultures, sometimes with strange results (how many names have been incised into trees and school desks as love charms attempting to establish the presence of the beloved?). When the Old English charm was directed into pasture land rather than plowed land, it required four sods taken before dawn from four sides of the enchanted field: the sods were blessed in various ways which mixed the old Germanic magic with the newer magic of Christianity and then returned to the field. But as each sod was replaced, fertility was further encouraged by burying under the sod a small cross of aspen wood with the names of Matthew, Mark, Luke, and John inscribed on the ends. And again there is another side of this power: Robert C. Elliott reminds us of the curse tablets (*defixiones*) of the Greeks and Romans, metal tablets buried in the earth or thrown into the sea, some with elaborate curses written on them, others bearing down with them only the name of the enemy with a nail driven through it (*The Power of Satire,* pp. 287-88).

In Dobuan magic the secret names of mythological forces are important elements in charms for fertility, for love, and for killing an enemy. The charms in general draw on three necessary powers—magic words, magic ritual, and magic naming—and though particular charms may emphasize one power and omit another, all three are felt to be fundamental to charm-magic. As in other charms, moreover, these powers in Dobuan charms are directed at two primary effects, which the sorcerers call *egoyainina* ("the naming and hurling away of evil") and *ebwainina* ("the naming and superimposing of good"—*Sorcerers of Dobu,* pp. 95, 129, 227). Evil (blights and pests in the gardens, a rival in love, an enemy in sorcery) is named to hurl it away, and good (growth of the yams, the beauty of the beloved, deadly powers and their effects on the enemy) is named to bring it here.

If in riddles names are the consequences of things—to name is to have known, and to know is to have seen—then in the charms things are a consequence of names, called forth by powers residing in names "from the beginning." Control of those powers depends not on clear vision but on obscure, esoteric knowledge, traditional or personal, which no amount of vision alone can uncover. There are riddles in the charm root, not the riddles defined by folklorists as "true riddles" but questions that are ultimately meant to deceive, enigmatic puzzles which only someone in possession of the secret knowledge can unravel. Folk literature is full of situations, often perilous ones, in which the power of this kind of naming survives. A "neck riddle" is a question asked by a condemned person which cannot be answered without the secret knowledge he alone possesses, and it gives him the power to save his life. In the folktale "Rumpelstiltskin" a mother is able to save her baby from a dwarf only after she secretly obtains the dwarf's name, and in the ballad "Riddles Wisely Expounded" (Child No. 1c) a girl drives away the Devil by naming him:

> As sune as she the fiend did name,
> He flew awa in a blazing flame.

We arrive, finally, at the second sense in which poetry can make things present by naming them. At the roots of phanopoeia, naming is a structure of vision and knowledge, and phanopoeia's way of making things present is to bring time and process into the present tense of the Image. At the roots of melopoeia, naming is a power directed at causing effects, bringing things from there to here or hurling them from here to there. The counterpart to the feeling of phanopoeia in our double sense of the Greek verb οἶδα is the double sense in the English verb "call," which means both "to name" and "to summon." The yams in their gardens, the Dobuans say, "grow big for our calling on them" (*Sorcerers of Dobu*, p. 107). Poetry is of course art and not magic, but when the charm root strongly informs the words of a lyric poem it commands a kind of attention quite different from the intellectual precision that a generation of critics trained on the metaphysical poets has learned to use. Ferdinand felt the charm-powers in Ariel's song without "figuring" it out. The two kinds of naming in poetry correspond to two different ways of charging the language of poems with meaning, and they appear to derive from very different roots. Both roots of lyric, we have agreed, lie in language, but in language itself lie even deeper sources, ways of seeing and powers of action.

VII. CHANT

THE MELOPOEIA of charms, as Huxley, Valéry, and the
Trobriand Islanders have pointed out to us, uses the irregular internal rhythms of the sounds in magic words for
purposes of magic action. Although no definite rules or firm
categories apply for long among the richly complex forms
of primitive poetry, beneath the complexities we can hear
and distinguish another rhythm in the melopoeia of this
poetry, a fundamentally different rhythm directed at a different kind of action. It is the root of our first kind of melopoeia, in which the external rhythms of music organize and
direct the words of a song. A regular rather than an irregular rhythm, it is based on pure, physical pulsation, the
kind of time-pattern that made Valéry wish for a musician's
gifts. We can experience rhythm without language, and can
easily imagine rhythm that is in fact prior to language. If
the street he was climbing had been less steep, Valéry could
have danced, for human art expresses such rhythms first
with dance and drum. And when such rhythms, essentially
independent of language, enter language, we have song.
In societies primitive or non-primitive, song is an art in
which the words are strongly controlled by rhythms derived from music and dance.

Primitive songs sung primarily for pleasure and enter-
tainment seem mainly to use the ordinary language of everyday speech, but the language is always subservient to the
musical rhythm. In contrast to the language of charms, we
find in the songs of many cultures words and syllables that
are truly "nonsense" sounds, or rather sounds which make
only rhythmical sense. They are not magic words directed
at magic actions, but rhythmical actions—sounds used as

time-makers, as part of the rhythmical pulse. Song-melos is a fundamentally heavier and more regular rhythm than charm-melos, and the charm's sound-repetitions of alliteration, assonance, rhyme, and repeated words tend to be more consistently patterned when they appear in song, often used to support larger units of repetition such as the verse-line or groups of lines in catalogues and refrains. Underlying and controlling all these repetitions of sound we can hear the pure beat of a dance rhythm.

Some of these rhythmical characteristics are heard in a song from the Eskimos of the Coppermine River. The song is about the hunter's bow; I quote only the first stanza in the native language, and the collector's literal translation of the entire song:

Verse 1.   pigiava nakigikpakpa
                picikcagyuk nakigikpakpa ai ya
Refrain.   pigiava i yai ya i ai yai yai ya
                pigiava i ai yai yai yai yai
Connective. i yai i yai

He constantly bends it, he constantly sends it straight,
The big bow, he constantly sends it straight.
He constantly bends it, i yai ya i ai yai yai ya,
He constantly bends it, i ai yai yai yai yai,
i yai i yai.

Subject-matter for words [theme for a song] as he really
    seeks well,
The big bow, he constantly sends it straight.
He constantly bends it, i yai ya i ai yai yai ya,
He constantly bends it, i ai yai yai yai yai,
i yai i yai.

He constantly bends it as he walks along,
In summer as he walks along.
He constantly bends it, i yai ya i ai yai yai ya,
He constantly bends it, i ai yai yai yai yai,
i yai i yai.

163

Big birds it is evidently easy to secure,
As he carries his pack, walking along.
He constantly bends it, i yai ya i ai yai yai ya,
He constantly bends it, i ai yai yai yai yai.

(Songs of the Copper Eskimos, pp. 459-60)

The song is actually danced and the dance rhythm is primary, the repeated sounds, repeated words, and repeated phrases all functioning as elements of that rhythm. And as in many dance songs, the rhythm in this song overrides language to the point of producing a large proportion of "meaningless" elements. The repeated *i yai* syllables are not magic words but, like our own culture's "too-ra-la" or "do-wop do-wah," rhythmical units, signs of the domination of language by music.

A dance song such as the Eskimo song is both a communal performance and a communal participation, and it is in this social context that we find a deeper basis for the rhythms of song-melos. Charms are generally not meant to be shared by a community. Rasmussen noted that Eskimo charms are usually performed in solitude, perhaps in the early morning before anyone else has walked on the floor, or outside in a remote place where there are no footprints of other men. The words of a charm are a closely guarded secret, the property of their owner; he may sell the charm, but its magic then goes with the new owner (*The Netsilik Eskimos*, p. 278). The suspicious Dobuans also guard their charms carefully, R. F. Fortune wrote, and any eavesdropper is regarded as a potential thief (*Sorcerers of Dobu*, p. 96). The nearby Trobriand Islanders appear to be more open about their charms, but this is because of their rigid respect for each other's property: one simply does not trespass on another's magic (*Coral Gardens and Their Magic*, II, 224-25). Cherokee sorcerers were freer with their charms for good hunting, love, or curing than with malevolent charms for hurting or killing, which they would not reveal to an uninitiated person at any price. Even in the case of charms for causing good, however, they worried that the magic became weaker the more it was diffused (*The Swimmer Manuscript*, pp. 147-48).

But alongside such privately owned and closely guarded charms are found charms that have moved into a more public area. Certain healing charms may be the property of secret societies, and this is a step closer to a communal context. The Trobriand garden-charms are the property of matrilineal kinship-groups, but their effect is a matter of concern for the whole community, and Malinowski tells us that the charms are overheard by most members of the community as the magician works for their benefit. For some Eskimo charms against blizzards, which threaten the entire community with famine, every member of the tribe is gathered to chant under the leadership of a shaman (*Songs of the Copper Eskimos*, p. 14). In a case such as this, the charm is likely to take on some of the rhythm of communal dance and song.

The rhythm of a song such as the Eskimo dance song is a communal rhythm, for the communal context of the song influences the rhythm in several ways. Since the song is meant to be danced by the members of the community, it demands a regular rhythm even if that rhythm has to be stretched over nonsense syllables. Communal participation also creates the regular refrain: the main verses are sung by a leader, but all the dancers sing the refrain. Beyond these direct influences are other communal associations, forces which in Copper Eskimo society focus on the dance hall as the center of social life and social action. The closed, internal rhythms and the special language of charms are meant for secret power, but the dance rhythms of primitive song are a public power which joins together the members of a society. Both are forms of action, one sacred and the other secular.

We find in primitive poetry, then, two distinguishable, but not always clearly separated, roots of melopoeia: the rhythms of charm-melos based in magic action and the rhythms of song-melos based in social action. They are found combined in a more complex form of literature which we may call—only for the purposes of distinction, and only in a very provisional mood—chant. It is poetry organized by both the internal rhythms of language and the external rhythms of music. Many chants are in fact danced, but even when they are not they retain a strong dance-rhythm, often reinforced by accompanying drums, rattles, tapping-sticks, or foot-stamps. The charm root is also present in the sound-associations of words, in many elements from a special language outside the language of everyday speech, and in the basis of sacred action—but here delivered as the voice of the society and acting for the benefit of the community.

The fullest realization of the communal context of chant is probably best represented by the impressive mythological chants associated with rituals that re-enact a tribal charter and reaffirm a communal identity. Such a chant comes from the Night Chant of the Navahos, a great healing ceremonial which gathers the entire community together. In this ceremonial, songs, dances, rites, and prayers are combined in one long ritual performed over a succession of nine nights and ten days for curing a diseased or injured member of the community. On the morning of the fourth day the shaman and the patient sit together in the medicine lodge and chant this prayer, the patient repeating the words line by line after the shaman:

Tse'gíhi
Hayolkál behogán
Nahotsoí behogán
Kósdilyil behogán
5 Niltsabaká behogán
Á'dilyil behogán
Niltsabaád behogán
Taditdín behogán
Aniltani behogán

10   Kósdilyil dadinlá'
      Kósdilyil biké dzeétin
      Atsinitlís yíke dasizíni
      Hastsébaka
      Nigél islá'
15   Nadíhila'
      Siké saádilil
      Sitsát saádilil
      Sitsís saáditlil
      Síni saáditlil
20   Siné saáditlil
      Tádisdzin naalíl sáhadilel
      Naalíl sahanéinla'
      Sitsádze tahíndinla'
      Nizágo nastlín
25   Hozógo nadedisdál
      Hozógo sitáha dinokél
      Hozógo tsidisál
      Sitáha honezkázigo nasádo
      Dosatéhigo nasádo
30   Dosohodilnígo nasádo
      Saná' nislíngo nasádo
      Daalkída kitégo nasádo
      Hozógo kósdilyil senahotlédo nasádo
      Hozógo nasádo
35   Hozógo sedahwiltíndo nasádo
      Hozógo nánise senahotlédo nasádo
      Hozógo taditdín keheetíngo nasádo
      Hozógo nasádo
      Tasé alkídzi ahonílgo nasádo
40   Sitsídze hozódo
      Sikéde hozódo
      Siyáde hozódo
      Sikide hozódo
      Siná taáltso hozódo
45   Hozó nahastlín
      Hozó nahastlín

Tse'gíhi.
House made of the dawn.
House made of evening light.
House made of the dark cloud.
5 House made of male rain.
House made of dark mist.
House made of female rain.
House made of pollen.
House made of grasshoppers.
10 Dark cloud is at the door.
The trail out of it is dark cloud.
The zigzag lightning stands high up on it.
Male deity!
Your offering I make.
15 I have prepared a smoke for you.
Restore my feet for me.
Restore my legs for me.
Restore my body for me.
Restore my mind for me.
20 Restore my voice for me.
This very day take out your spell for me.
Your spell remove for me.
You have taken it away for me.
Far off it has gone.
25 Happily I recover.
Happily my interior becomes cool.
Happily I go forth.
My interior feeling cool, may I walk.
No longer sore, may I walk.
30 Impervious to pain, may I walk.
With lively feelings may I walk.
As it used to be long ago, may I walk.
Happily may I walk.
Happily with abundant dark clouds, may I walk.
35 Happily with abundant showers, may I walk.
Happily with abundant plants, may I walk.
Happily on a trail of pollen, may I walk.

Happily may I walk.
Being as it used to be long ago, may I walk.
40 May it be happy [or beautiful] before me.
May it be beautiful behind me.
May it be beautiful below me.
May it be beautiful above me.
May it be beautiful all around me.
45 In beauty it is finished.
In beauty it is finished.[1]

Charm-melos and song-melos come together in the rhythms of this prayer. The words of a prayer operate in the context of religion in a manner analogous to the verbal actions of a charm in the context of magic, and the sound-patterns we expect to hear in a charm occur here as well. There is the word-repetition of *behogán* ("house made of . . .") in what we might call the invocation (vv. 1-15), and the same device is used with other words throughout the prayer. In the section that beseeches the god to remove sickness or disease (vv. 16-22) a sound-pattern is built up through the incantation of repeated *s* sounds (*Siké . . . Sitsát . . . Sitsís . . . Síni . . . Siné*), and at the end of the prayer this pattern also recurs (vv. 40-44). As charms are accompanied by ritual actions, this prayer is accompanied by the application of pollen to parts of the patient's body and by the sacrifice of sacred bundles to the gods.

From our point of view, however, the prayer is more chant than charm. The sound-repetitions and word-repetitions are part of more regular patterns that form the verse-line into a single rhythmical unit repeated not rigidly but regularly, most obviously in the repetition of each line by the patient and in the several striking catalogues. The steady regularity of the patterns of repeated sounds, words, and lines is a clue to the underlying dance rhythm of the chant. The prayer is not danced and not sung, but the rhythms of Navaho dance-song, which follow the steady beat of rattle and basket-drum, are still strongly felt. Forms

of the same prayer are addressed to different gods throughout the entire ceremonial of the Night Chant, and on the
ninth day it is chanted publicly with dancers actually present, keeping up a restrained but constant dance-rhythm
with their feet and bodies.[2]

Although such signs of song-melos are evident in the
prayer itself, its power of social action becomes apparent
only when it is considered in its communal context. Washington Matthews, who studied and recorded the Night
Chant ceremonial, observed that it is a great social event for
the Navahos, a time for the people to gather together to
socialize, feast, gamble, and race horses, but also to act as
witnesses to the dances and rituals. The ceremonial itself
is primarily concerned with curing a particular individual
of disease or injury, but its prayers also invoke the gods for
happiness, abundant rains, good crops, and other blessings
for the community as a whole. In traditional societies religion is a central element of communal identity, and in
the course of the Night Chant nearly all the important
gods and spirits of the Navahos are mentioned in its myths,
songs, and prayers, depicted in its sand-paintings, or represented by its masqueraders (*The Night Chant*, pp. 3-4).
The central myth of the Night Chant relates the journey of
The Visionary, a man who traveled with the gods, learned
the ceremonial from them, and brought back its powers of
healing and fertility to the Navaho people. Through the
rituals of the ceremonial, the shaman and the patient—
with the tribe as witness—symbolically re-enact the myth of
the journey, and the cure, it has been suggested, is effected
by submerging the patient in the primal sources of tribal
identity embodied in this basic myth.[3] The formula at the
end of the prayer of the fourth day, and all the other prayers like it, is *Hozó nahastlín*: it means, according to Matthews, "It is done in beauty" or "It is finished happily" and
is analogous to the Christian "amen" (*The Night Chant*, p.
296). In both formulas we hear communal recognition and
assent to the words of the prayer.

The dance rhythm and the powers of social action at the roots of mythological chants are seen again in an Aranda chant collected in Central Australia by T.G.H. Strehlow. Sections of the chant are at times danced, and at those times it is, like the Navaho chant, part of a full ritual drama. The dances re-enact the awakening and the bloody journey of Ankotarinja, the dingo (Australian wild dog)-ancestor of a totemic group. The origin myth associated with the chant and the rituals tells how Ankotarinja, after lying asleep for long ages in a hollow in the earth, slowly came to consciousness and arose from the soft soil. He covered himself with red down and sniffed the four winds, finding in the west wind the warm scent of *tjilpa* (native cat)-men. The scent angered him: he rushed through an underground journey and emerged in the west, where dog-like he tracked down the men and devoured them. Full to bursting, he lay down and fell asleep. There came upon the scene of the massacre another man, an avenger from the west who decapitated the sleeping Ankotarinja and released the swallowed men. But a totem-ancestor can never completely die, and the head of Ankotarinja rolled back through the underground passage to seek the hollow from which it first emerged, and there it finally came to rest.

The myth embodies the communal consciousness of the totemic group, and in the chant it is fused with the dance rhythm. In the ritual that re-enacts the myth, a central actor performs the actions of the dog-ancestor, furiously scratching the earth on all fours; the old men of the group chant the verses and keep up a steady rhythm by beating the ground with firebrands or boomerangs while the rest of the men perform a shuffling dance around him. Groups of lines are repeated over and over while the actor is being prepared and while he performs the ritual. The language of the chant is an extremely artificial language, completely dominated by external patterns of rhythm. The words of everyday language are broken up into syllables and rearranged according to formal, traditional patterns of versifi-

cation. Speech rhythm gives way to chant rhythm, yielding
a special chant language characterized by strong patterns
of repetition in sound, word, and verse-line:

1. Nómabaué rérlanopái
   Nómayatín tyélanopái
2. Nómabué rélanopái
   Nómaalbá tínyanopái
3. Nómabaué rérlanopái
   Nómatnyenyá lbélanopái
4. Nómaarkwé rkárlanopái
   Nómatnyenyá lbélanopái
5. Nómakanté kántanopái
   Nómatnyenyá lbélanopái
6. Tnímarubúrubá láitnibé
   Tnímawurúbingá láitnibé
7. Tnímanatán tyálitnibé
   Tnímawurúbingá láitnibé
8. Ratúwatelá lurbmáturatú
   Ralílertyalá lurbmáturatú
9. Watúwatelá lumbátnuwatnú
   Walílertyelá lumbátnuwatnú
10. Limanowó bintyintilé
    Limaldulé ratyintilé
11. Limangkulé ralintilé
    Limaldule ratyintile
12. Maramínyutikéle
    Naramínyutikéle,
    Nikwantálbantítyaló,
    Mikwantálbantítyaló
13. Marangkálurkngulyelé
    Mikwantélbantityaló
14. Warábityábityáu,
    Walyutulbélo

15. Ntimankoté namariré nalintibé
    Ntimaatyá ralintibé
16. Ntimatyibú larintibé
    Ntimaatyá ralintibé
17. Ntimangkulé ralintibé
    Ntimanuwo bintyintibe
18. Nómaarkwé rkárlanopái
    Nómatnyenyá lbélanopái

(Since the words are broken up and rearranged according to the verse patterns, the medial break is only a caesura, not a new word.) The translation, Strehlow says, is necessarily a free one that attempts to catch some of the shades of meaning in the original. Most of the words in the first five lines, for example, mean generally "are red" or "gleam red," yet they are all derived from different roots and carry different implications in the Aranda language:

1. Red is the down which is covering me;
   Red I am as though I was burning in a fire.
2. Red I am as though I was burning in a fire,
   Bright red gleams the ochre with which I have rubbed my body.
3. Red I am as though I was burning in a fire,
   Red, too, is the hollow in which I am lying.
4. Red I am like the heart of a flame of fire,
   Red, too, is the hollow in which I am lying.
5. The red tjurunga is resting upon my head,
   Red, too, is the hollow in which I am lying.
6. Like a whirlwind it is towering to the sky,
   Like a pillar of red sand it is towering to the sky.
7. The tnatantja is towering to the sky,
   Like a pillar of red sand it is towering to the sky.
8. A mass of red pebbles covers the plains,
   Little white sand-rills cover the plains.

9. Lines of red pebbles streak the plains,
   Lines of white sand-rills streak the plains.

10. An underground pathway lies open before me,
    Leading straight west, it lies open before me.

11. A cavernous pathway lies open before me,
    Leading straight west, it lies open before me.

12. He is sucking his beard into his mouth in anger,
    Like a dog he follows the trail by scent.

13. He hurries on swiftly, like a keen dog;
    Like a dog he follows the trail by scent.

14. Irresistible and foaming with rage,—
    Like a whirlwind he rakes them together.

15. Out yonder, not far from me, lies Ankota;
    The underground hollow is gaping open before me.

16. A straight track is gaping open before me,
    An underground hollow is gaping open before me.

17. A cavernous pathway is gaping open before me,
    An underground pathway is gaping open before me.

18. Red I am, like the heart of a flame of fire,
    Red, too, is the hollow in which I am resting.

(The *tnatantja* mentioned in the chant is a towering, living pole of great power conceived of as having risen from the totemic ground "ever from the beginning" and represented in the ceremonies by a tall, decorated wooden pole. *Tjurunga* refers generally to sacred stone or wooden objects infused with the power and fertility of the totemic ancestor, and in this chant refers specifically to the *tnatantja*. Ankota is the name of the totemic ground where Ankotarinja first emerged and where his head finally came to rest.)[4]

The rhythmical structures, patterns of versification, and special forms of language in this and other Aranda chants are complex and sophisticated, but the fundamental principle of rhythmical organization is a steady and regular musical measure. The chants, Strehlow writes, "owe most of their poetic form and interesting structure to the hammer-beats of the rhythms that ring through their couplets" (*Songs of Central Australia*, p. 18). We can probably get no closer than this Australian chant to the roots of the chant rhythm, and we can sense, though never prove, that the basis of that rhythm lies in the communal context, that it is a public power directed at social action. There are clear reasons why a communal chant or dance must be based on regular patterns of repetition, but, like the basis of the irregular charm-rhythm in magic, more interesting reasons lie deeper. The fact that a chant, particularly a mytho-logical chant, *needs* to be expressed in a regular rhythm, in a public rather than a private and secretive rhythm, comes from the purpose of the chant and the reason it came into existence.

The Aranda chant grew out of the shared knowledge of a totemic group, a knowledge which the chant in turn re-creates for the group. The entire ritual—the chant, the myth, the dance, the drama—is an explanation of the ori-gins of the totemic ancestor, and therefore of the group itself. The re-creation of this knowledge, then, is also a reaffirmation of the group's existence. The goal of the chant is an ambitious one: through the dance, through the social action of the ritual, through the shared knowledge of com-munal origins, it attempts to create and maintain a rhythm uniting individuals into a community. Rhythm, perhaps, can function in this manner only in a traditional society, or in those brief communities that form when individuals momentarily share a common knowledge, identity, and goal. Work songs, though rare in primitive societies, are common in folk cultures, and they necessarily show the same strong rhythmic movement and regular patterns of repetition. The game-songs of children and the songs and chants of football games or protest marches are further in-stances—trivial examples, it may seem, when compared to the Navaho and Australian chants, but nevertheless redis-coveries of an old and powerful root of poetry.

The melopoeia of poetry is usually approached through carefully defined and largely self-contained systems of prosody. At the roots, however, melopoeia is inseparable from much broader areas of human experience. Our subject is the rhythm of chants, but that rhythm directly involves us in speculations about myth and time, language and action, as deeper foundations of the music of poetry.

In place of phanopoeia's sense of pattern, of time caught in space, we hear in the chants a steady beat carrying the poetry forward through time and action. Quarles' *Hieroglyphics of the Life of Man* presented a method of phanopoeia that catches up the themes of time and process in picture and spatial form. The Navaho chant and the Aranda chant, on the other hand, present a poetry in which one of the roots of melopoeia, the underlying dance rhythm, is fused with the theme of a journey and its strong sense of movement. In the Navaho chant the dance rhythm is joined to The Visionary's archetypal journey to the gods for curative powers, in the Aranda chant to the furious, rushing journey of the ancestor Ankotarinja. Again, this is not simply onomatopoeia but two very different forms of expression working together. Yet the two forms of expression, rhythm and theme, both derive from fundamental bases in communal action. Behind the rhythm is the communal action of dance, and behind the themes are communal myths which emphasize movement.

The ethnologist Margot Astrov has suggested that the theme of traveling in Navaho myths is an important aspect of the social and cultural context from which the chants were formed. The creation myth of the Navahos, she writes, is a myth conceived primarily in terms of motion, an "emergence" of the people which they call *hijínai* ("moving upward"), and it is a myth of continual movement and transformation up through the Five Worlds. The myths associated with the healing ceremonials (Astrov mentions the Night Chant and the Mountain Chant in particular) are journey-myths in which a hero travels to find medicine and knowledge to bring back for the benefit of the people. But the myths give much more emphasis to the traveling than to the goal finally attained. The hero's journeys with all their dangers make up the bulk of these narratives, and the geography through which he passes is carefully described and precisely named. He receives his power, it becomes clear, not only from the medicine finally granted him by the gods he seeks but also from traveling itself. A key formula in the Mountain Chant and the Night Chant is *sa'a narái* (Matthews' *sáan nagaí*), translated by various collectors as "in old age wandering," "restoration to youth," or "the person who travels far and wide." It expresses, Astrov says, "all that seems most desirable, most perfect, most sacred to the Navaho":

> It is in accord with Navaho belief that a person whose very business it is to move becomes the symbol of the most sacred, the most powerful. It is the Traveler, after all, who meets the gods; it is the Traveler who, in suffering and ecstasy, finds the redeeming herb; it is the Traveler who, in venturing upon unknown trails, absorbs all those healing powers that are believed to dwell in things simply because they have been encountered in places unfamiliar and far distant. It seems logical, therefore, that the patient is made, ritual-symbolically, the traveler who reënacts the journeys of the first patient-traveler.[5]

The Navaho healing chants, we see, organize myth and ritual through a rhythm that carries the patient along the path of the original hero. The patient makes the journey again, yet at the same time he is the original Traveler on the original journey.

Our first speculation, then, concerns time and mythological action in the chants, and it is not limited to the Navahos. The mythological chants of the Navaho and the Aranda primarily express movement and action through time, but myth, we know, can do strange things with time. On a particular day and in a particular social context, a member of the society participates in a particular rhythm, a chant. Mythological action, however, can and is in fact meant to give the chant the power of transforming these events of the immediate context into something beyond the ordinary time of human experience. The native Australians call it "The Dreaming," their version of the mythic time-lessness which we approached through phanopoeia in Li Shang-yin's "Inlaid Harp" and Yeats's "Magi." R. M. Berndt, in discussing the sacred Kunapipi songs of north-eastern Arnhem Land, reports, "It is said that they are the actual songs sung by the Ancestral Beings in the 'Dreaming' era, that their rhythm and content stretch unbrokenly through the ages and on interminably into the future. Aborigines say: 'These songs are the echo of those first sung by the Wauwalak and the Kunapipi people; the spirit of the echo goes on through timeless space, and when we sing, we take up the echo and make sound.' "[6] In mythological chants, social action is fused with the sacred as curing and power are attained by contact with the primal roots of the tribe. It requires, and enforces, participation in the fullest sense of the word. The participant is a patient or an initiate—it will not act on us—and the rest of the community or totemic group are with him as witnesses. Through the chant they join a continuing rhythm and community, both of which "stretch unbrokenly through the ages and on inter-minably into the future." "Now as at all times," Yeats said; sa'a narái, the Navahos say. Myth approached through phanopoeia catches the transient moment of vision in time-less models, but approached through melopoeia it joins the rhythms of time and human experience to continuing rhythms of eternity.

A second speculation involves the roots of melopoeia with the nature of language itself. Mythological chants represent a special use of language which acts to cause a particular effect. The language of garden-magic also acts to cause a particular effect, and it appears to have been this use of language in the Trobriand Islands that led Bronislaw Malinowski to formulate a general theory of language based in action. An important theory in the history of anthropology, Malinowski's view of language also contributes to our present concerns.

The fundamental nature of language, Malinowski felt, is not to imitate thought but to act, to produce an effect. Language does not *represent* mental concepts but *is* a physical action and process: "The fact is that the main function of language is not to express thought, not to duplicate mental processes, but rather to play an active pragmatic part in human behaviour" (*Coral Gardens and Their Magic*, ii, 7). The basic function of the language of everyday speech, in our own culture as well as in pre-literate cultures, is to "connect work and correlate manual and bodily movements. Words are part of action and they are equivalents to actions." In their different realm, the words of the special language of magic are also actions, and charms are not, to the people who use them, pieces of literature. A charm is rather "a verbal act by which a specific force is let loose—an act which in native belief exercises the most powerful influence on the course of nature and on human behaviour" (ii, 9). The meaning of an ordinary sentence or of a magic charm, then, lies far less in any mental concepts attached to the words than in their function and effect. Meaning cannot be defined in a dictionary or an ethnologist's glossary, but only within what Malinowski called the "context of situation" and the "context of culture." When a word is used it is always used within these contexts, and when a word is not being used it simply does not exist: "The speech of a pre-literate community brings home to us in an unavoidably cogent manner that language exists only in actual use within the context of real utterance" (ii, vii). Although these few fragments do not do justice to Malinowski's complete presentation of his theory of language, they demonstrate clearly that we are dealing with a theory that views the roots of language as essentially, and in fact exclusively, pragmatic.

We seem to be in the business of recovering abandoned theories of language for the service of poetics. In doing so, we are in a sense still following Wordsworth. But ordinary speech, "the language really spoken by men" in everyday conversation, is only one source of the poet's language, and the kinds of language envisioned by a Fenollosa or a Malinowski can be realized in the language of poetry. Fenollosa the art historian projected a general theory of language in terms of phanopoeia and the visual ideogram; seeing and knowing and naming have left deep roots in language, and these roots, he felt, can be rediscovered and reactivated by a poet's careful use of his language. Malinowski the anthropologist of magic projected a pragmatic theory of language, and his theory suggests to us a poetics based on the possibilities in language for magic action and social action. They are roots carried in language primarily in terms of melopoeia, and we have found in our discussion of the rhythms of charms and chants that the roots of melopoeia are deeply connected with ideas of action. The charm rhythm is an internal rhythm arising from the necessity for words which move, and the more complex chant rhythm joins this movement with the stronger, external movements of music and dance to effect social action. These uses of language have also left roots for poets to recover, roots which bring with them not vision but power. From Fenollosa, then, we derive a poetics of "deep mimesis," and from Malinowski a poetics of "deep praxis." The Greek words themselves may remind us that both uses of language were concerns of Plato—mimesis, which he disparaged, and praxis, which he feared—and that together Fenollosa and Malinowski finally describe the language poets have always known.

Another form of chant, particularly powerful in expressing a sense of movement and social action, is the prophecy.

The dance rhythms and strong, repetitive catalogues of all chants are heard in prophecies, but they are often pushed to a kind of speed limit by the prophecy's feeling of pressure and urgency. Elements of the charm rhythm also appear here, but prophecy is deeply involved in a communal context, and the rhythm of prophecy is mainly the communal rhythm of chant rather than the more individual rhythm of charm. Although a prophecy may often have its source in an individual dream or vision, the individual who travels in vision brings back a report for the benefit of the community, and the vision is quickly assimilated to the communal expression of chant. As part of this communal orientation, prophecy associates itself very easily with public lament, and the two forms are often found blended into one.

In the 1890's James Mooney was able to collect from several American Indian tribes the songs of the Ghost Dance. As a messianic movement the Ghost Dance tended naturally toward prophecies of the better world coming to the Indian, and as a nativistic movement it included just as naturally laments for the impoverished present and the loss of former days—days when things were better, before the coming of the white men. The Ghost Dance functioned as a healing ceremony for entire communities, and the songs are deeply rooted in the communal consciousness. The rhythms are communal rhythms: drums and rattles were not used, but with the exception of the invocation the songs were still danced, and Mooney noted that their rhythms were all "adapted to the simple measure of the dance step."[7] Along with the dance rhythms are the regular patterns of repetition. Most Ghost Dance songs repeated each line, the song as a whole was repeated over and over while the dance progressed, and the "songs" are, in effect, long chants. The journey motif is here dramatically combined with the dance rhythm, for one of the functions of the dance was to induce a dancer into a trance during which his body fell to the ground and he traveled in vision to the spirit world. Most of the songs were composed by dancers as reports of what they saw in their visions.

One of the conditions for a messianic movement is that a community find itself in an intolerable state, one usually involving, among other things, poverty, humiliation, and a sense of helplessness. An Arapaho song from the Ghost Dance is primarily a lament describing the Indians' feeling of wretchedness. It is a pathetic song, and Mooney noted that sometimes tears would roll down the dancers' cheeks as they shared the knowledge of their misery:

> Aníqu néchawúnaní,
> Aníqu néchawúnaní;
> Awáwa biqanákayéna,
> Awáwa biqanákayéna;
> Iyahúh níbithíti,
> Iyahúh níbithíti.

> Father, have pity on me,
> Father, have pity on me;
> I am crying for thirst,
> I am crying for thirst;
> All is gone—I have nothing to eat,
> All is gone—I have nothing to eat.

> (p. 977)

The world to come, the spirit world visited by the dancers in their trances, was also the world that had once been. All the Ghost Dance songs recall the age before the coming of the white men as the model for the age which is to come, and the songs often dwell on details of this former age. A hunter leaving for a hunt calls for his bow rather than a rifle; a woman meets old friends from her childhood and together they play a game which has long since passed out of use; a dreamer sees the women in the spirit world preparing pemmican, formerly a favorite food of the prairie tribes:

CHANT

Nátanúya chébính—
Nátanúya chébính,
Náchichábán,
Náchichábán.

The pemmican that I am using—
The pemmican that I am using,
They are still making it,
They are still making it.　　　(p. 991)

Although this is a dance song, there is an undeniable charm
quality in the clusters of *na* and *ch* sounds. There is, moreover, a sense of magic—but a communal sense, lying in the
importance of the Indians' rediscovery of this one small
sign of their communal identity. "They are still making it"
is the prophecy, the promise that this identity will become
strong once again.

Pemmican was dried and pounded buffalo meat, and one
of the most significant prophecies of the Ghost Dance was
the return of the great buffalo herds. The buffalo had been
the basis of the Plains Indian economy, and it occupied a
central position in their traditions and rituals. The return
of the buffalo not only promised the Indians a return to
power, but it also signified the return of an element woven
deeply into their tribal consciousness. The following Sioux
song is such a prophecy. Through the messages brought to
the tribe by the sacred birds, the eagle and the crow, it sees
in the returning buffalo the return of the community itself:

Maká sitómaniyan ukiye,
Oyáte ukíye, oyáte ukíye,
Wánbali oyáte wan hoshíhi-ye lo,
Ate heye lo, ate heye lo,
Maka ówancháya ukíye.
Pte kin ukiye, pte kin ukiye,
Kanghi oyáte wan hoshíhi-ye lo,
Áte héye lo, áte héye lo.

183

The whole world is coming,
A nation is coming, a nation is coming,
The Eagle has brought the message to the tribe.
The father says so, the father says so.
Over the whole earth they are coming.
The buffalo are coming, the buffalo are coming,
The Crow has brought the message to the tribe,
The father says so, the father says so. (p. 1072)

This song catches the rushing movement, the feeling of events sweeping down on us, for which prophecy is especially suitable. It is the melopoeic sense of movement and propulsion heard in the Aranda chant as well, and something quite different from the patterned sense of thought found, for example, in the emblem. Many of the Ghost Dance prophecies express this strong sense of movement, and in this striking Paiute song it is foreshortened by acceleration to the point of apocalypse:

Wumbíndomán, Wumbíndomán,
Wumbíndomán, Wumbíndomán.
Nuváríp noyówaná, Nuváríp noyówaná,
Nuváríp noyówaná, Nuváríp noyówaná.

The whirlwind! The whirlwind!
The whirlwind! The whirlwind!
The snowy earth comes gliding, the snowy earth comes
gliding;
The snowy earth comes gliding, the snowy earth comes
gliding. (p. 1054)

Like other forms of melopoeia, prophecy is based on oral expression, but it can nevertheless appear in a highly literate civilization, as the examples of Jeremiah and Isaiah show. A final example of prophecy comes from the Mayas of the Yucatan, a literate civilization but one that appears also to have retained a strong sense of communal identity. Prophecy occupied an important place in Maya literature, and probably the greatest Maya prophet that we will ever

CHANT

know of was the last, Chilam Balam, who lived at the end
of the fifteenth and the beginning of the sixteenth centuries.
When the Spanish arrived shortly after, their missionaries
destroyed the sacred books of the Mayas, which were recorded in hieroglyphic writing, and taught the Indians to
write using a European script adapted to the Mayan language. It is in this form that the prophecies of Chilam
Balam have reached us. Knowledge of the hieroglyphic writing began to die, but a few of the Chilam Balam books,
secretly copied and recopied in the new alphabetic writing
in the villages of the Yucatan, managed to survive the book-
burnings of the missionaries and to reach the twentieth
century. The following prophecy is not, therefore, from
a primitive culture but from a literate civilization, yet the
central elements of primitive chant are still very much in
use. The actual dancing of chant is gone, but a steady
rhythm persists in the strong repetitions of *Tu kin* ("on
that day") which beat at the beginnings of eleven lines in
a row, and in the catalogue of coming disasters. Here
prophecy is also lament, and the two are tied to the sense
of community. The approaching doom is not for just one
man but for whole generations of a society. The strong sense
of rushing events seen in the last two Ghost Dance songs is
here as well: the people are told to seize the day, to eat and
drink while they still have bread and water, for a day is
fast rushing upon them when these necessary elements of
life, and with them the life of the civilization as a whole,
will be lost:

> Uien, uien, a man uah;
> Uken, uken, a man haa;
> Tu kin, puz lum pach,
> Tu kin, tzuch lum ich,
> Tu kin, naclah muyal,
> Tu kin, naclah uitz,
> Tu kin, chuc lum dziic,
> Tu kin, hubulhub,

185

Tu kin, codz yol chelem,
Tu kin, edzeledz,
Tu kin, ox dzalab u nak yaxche,
Tu kin, ox chuilab xotem,
Tu kin, pan tzintzin
Yetel banhob yalan che yalan haban.

Eat, eat, thou hast bread;
Drink, drink, thou hast water;
On that day, dust possesses the earth,
On that day, a blight is on the face of the earth,
On that day, a cloud rises,
On that day, a mountain rises,
On that day, a strong man seizes the land,
On that day, things fall to ruin,
On that day, the tender leaf is destroyed,
On that day, the dying eyes are closed,
On that day, three signs are on the tree,
On that day, three generations hang there,
On that day, the battle flag is raised,
And they [i.e., the people] are scattered afar in the
     forests.[8]

Like the Ghost Dance songs, Chilam Balam's prophecies
originated in an individual trance, but they expressed in the
rhythms of the communal voice matters which concerned
the entire society. This prophecy, apparently from the first
or second decade of the sixteenth century, probably referred
to the return from the east of Quetzalcoatl, known to the
Mayas as Kukulcan. It was the Spanish, however, who were
already in the West Indies, and whose landings in the
Yucatan in 1527 brought the prophecy dramatic confirma-
tion.

Primitive chant, like other basic forms, sometimes appears whole and untransformed in the midst of the most
sophisticated poetic traditions. Although the association
with dance has been left behind, the communal basis still

exists in such forms as temple-chanting and church litanies, and some poets have used these forms as roots in their own poetry. In general, however, the attempts of literate poets in a modern civilization—Vachel Lindsay, for example— to catch the communal rhythm have produced little that could be mistaken for serious poetry. Such attempts are conscious literary imitations, and their rhythms do not grow out of a basis in community. T. S. Eliot reached toward this rhythm in experiments with music-hall rhythms, suggesting, perhaps, that for us the expression of a communal rhythm is better fitted to drama than to lyric poetry. There are of course exceptions to prove the rule, and the Whitman of "Crossing Brooklyn Ferry" and "Song of Myself" comes to mind. But Whitman's chant rhythm often loses motion as its dance falters or stops. We would most expect to hear this rhythm, with its repetitions and catalogues and its rushing, prophetic voice, in his lament for Lincoln, a poem which attempted to speak for a nation. But we often find instead static lines and catalogues which, rather than pushing forward, circle back to fill in the details of a picture:

> Now while I sat in the day and look'd forth,
> In the close of the day with its light and the fields of
>   spring, and the farmers preparing their crops,
> In the large unconscious scenery of my land with its
>   lakes and forests. . . .
>   ("When Lilacs Last in the Dooryard Bloom'd")

In modern poetry the communal rhythm has become even fainter, and modern poets tend toward a language that emphasizes other things: the Image rather than a rushing rhythm; the precision of careful thought rather than repetition, catalogue, or incantation; autonomy and impersonality rather than the *participation mystique* of the communal voice. The root is still present, however, and every now and then a modern poem will surprise us with a sudden emergence of that basic, communal voice. Whatever reservations literary critics may now have about Allen Ginsberg's "Howl," there are people who are not likely to forget that strong sense of identification felt when in the mid-1950's the poem first burst out of San Francisco. It had the rushing rhythms, the strong repetitions and catalogues; it was part of a movement of poetry meant to be chanted aloud in readings that sometimes became violently, if not mystically, participatory; it spoke with a communal voice and was both a prophecy and a lament for that community:

> I saw the best minds of my generation destroyed by madness, starving hysterical naked,
> dragging themselves through the negro streets at dawn looking for an angry fix,
> angelheaded hipsters burning for the ancient heavenly connection to the starry dynamo in the machinery of night,
> who poverty and tatters and hollow-eyed and high sat up smoking in the supernatural darkness of cold-water flats floating across the tops of cities contemplating jazz. . . .[9]

Ginsberg is still at it, of course, now accompanying his chants with the rhythms of small iron rings and finger-cymbals. The influence is probably from the mantram-chanting of India, yet the result is not far from the Australian using his tapping-sticks or the Navaho his basket-drum to propel the rhythms of their great mythological chants.

Somewhat different examples of the chant rhythm are the later poems of Imamu Amiri Baraka (LeRoi Jones). They are involved enough in the context of social action to have been used against him in January, 1968, as evidence in a trial.[10] It is easy to pick out their poetic roots: they are public curses and prophecies and calls to action built on the melopoeia of a pulsing, rushing beat, repetition and catalogue, and, most importantly in this case, the communal rhythms of a "street voice" that can bring his audiences to their feet in recognition and identity. Generally, however, chant remains more important as a root than as an actual poetic form. The aural imagination which could once find delight in the repetitive rhythms of a catalogue has declined, as has the strong sense of community which could be called up and reinforced by communal namings—genealogies, lists of gods, ancestors, or tribal heroes, and catalogues of familiar place-names. The communal participation of a tribal dance usually exists only as an historical explanation and not as a formal cause of this rhythm, and the necessary condition of a communal identity is fading fast even where it does exist. Ethnologists are hard-pressed to find the old men in an Australian or Navaho tribe who still remember the complete chants, and even the "street-voice" rhythms of Baraka may not last long as his community fragments and turns from an oral culture to a print culture. Yet the roots remain carried in the language, capable of feeding and transforming the work of individual poets who, pushing for movement in their poems, suddenly hear the repetitions and movements of that dance-beat.

VIII. RHYTHM

IN THE Preface to the *Lyrical Ballads* Wordsworth stated boldly that there is no essential difference between the language of poetry and the language of good prose. Yet he took some pains to justify one inessential difference, the use of metrical language in poetry. In the context of the Preface, with its emphasis on the language really spoken by men, his defense of meter is a strange one, for all the benefits he sees arising from the use of meter in poetry depend on a recognition of its artificiality. If the poet is accurately describing the great and universal passions of men, the activities of men, and the world in which men live, meter can add "charm" to those descriptions; if the feelings of the poet become too strong and are in danger of being carried beyond their proper bounds, the presence of regular meter will temper and restrain those feelings "by an intertexture of ordinary feeling, and of feeling not strictly and necessarily connected with the passion"; if, on the other hand, the poet's language is inadequate for the occasion and is unable to reach the heights that the passion demands, the meter will help by bringing traditional associations to the particular subject, feelings which the reader "has been accustomed to connect with metre in general" and cheerful or melancholy feelings "which he has been accustomed to connect with that particular movement of metre." The general principle at work here is, as Wordsworth clearly saw, "the tendency of metre to divest language, in a certain degree, of its reality." The language of poetry, he said, closely resembles, yet widely differs from, the language of real life, and this "similitude in dissimilitude" is the basis of the pleasure we feel in a poet's skillful use of metrical language. Wordsworth had already reached a profound level of discussion here—one involving not only the basis of meter but the basis of all mimetic art and of much that is significant in human experience generally—when he turned aside, deciding that it lay beyond the limits of a simple preface.

There are in general two interesting versions of the roots of poetic meter. One approach, the one taken by Wordsworth and by many before him, traces meter back to the rhythms of speech. The best modern presentation of this view has been made by John Thompson in *The Founding of English Metre* (London: Routledge and Kegan Paul, 1961). Using the researches of linguists into the nature of the spoken language, Thompson writes that meter is an abstract model of certain essential features in the language of everyday speech. In English, those essential features are the phonemic qualities of segmental phonemes (vowels and consonants), stress, pitch, and juncture. English meter is a patterned imitation that emphasizes one of these features, stress, in particular, though finally it is a model of the ways in which all these elements work in the spoken language:

> Metre is made by abstracting from speech one of these essential features and ordering this into a pattern. The pattern is an imitation of the patterns that the feature makes in speech, a sort of formalizing of these patterns. Actually the metrical pattern represents not only the one feature it is based on but all the essential features of the language. And in organizing these into its abstract patterns, metre follows the principles of our language with the utmost precision. Perhaps it has always been apparent that the elements of metre are drawn from the language. Gascoigne observed this . . . and the scholar Paul Verrier, writing on English metre, said that both poetry and song derive their rhythms and their melody from the language. (p. 11)

For Thompson, the patterns of traditional foot-prosody (iambic, trochaic, etc.) are a good basis for the notation of English meter. However confused the ancestry of these patterns may be, they are a working system that poets have known and used, and they have come to represent actual patterns of stress in the spoken language.

The other version of the roots of poetic meter traces them back to the rhythms of song rather than speech. Since Wordsworth's poet is a man speaking, not singing, to men, this view does not come up in the Preface. It is, however, another old and long-respected theory, and it too continues to flourish. M. W. Croll, who saw meter as poetry's heritage from song, represents one example of this approach. The roots of meter, he felt, lie in those external rhythms that have always been used to form language to the measures of music:

> The rhythmic form of verse is the same in its essential principles as that of the music of song, from which it is, in fact, derived in the first instance. In some kinds of verse, it is true, the form is much more remote from that of song than in others. For example, our English blank verse and the French Alexandrine line have been made, more or less deliberately, as unlike song as verse can ever be; and indeed all verse meant to be used in long poems or to be spoken in anything like the level of tone of prose discourse must have been treated in the same way. Still, the changes that have been introduced into our "spoken" verse, as we may call it, have not affected the fundamental principles of rhythm which it derives from song; they are merely additional procedures which restrict the operation of these principles within certain limits, without changing them in any way or adding new ones to them. Meanwhile a great deal of poetry continues and will always continue to be made as much like song as possible. Dancing and

music are the arts of rhythm; they have nothing to learn about their own business from poetry; poetry, on the other hand, has derived all it knows about rhythm from them. The best way to approach the study of the rhythm of verse, therefore, is by way of the form of song.[1]

Poetic meter is seen here as fundamentally musical "measure," and it is best notated by time signatures, bar lines, notes which indicate syllable duration, and rests.

Both versions of poetic meter recognize that a metrical pattern does not tell us the whole story of the rhythm in a line of poetry. In fact, the most valued effects of meter in poetry occur not when the language corresponds with docile regularity to the metrical pattern, but on those occasions when rhythms in the language challenge and conflict with that regular pattern. In Shakespeare, Donne, Milton, or Keats the meter is most interesting to us when there is some interplay between the pattern and other rhythms in the language. This effect was called *counterpoint* by Hopkins; critics using traditional metrics often call it simply *tension*, and critics who tend toward a "musical" system of meter prefer the more specific *syncopation*. Although Hopkins was more subtle, or more elusive, in his discussion of "counterpoint," it is usually described as the combined effect of the regular metrical pattern and the variable rhythms of speech—a resultant, we might say, of the force of the meter and the forces of the normal movements in the spoken language. In Croll's "musical" system it occurs whenever the rhythms of speech cause a stress to fall either before or after the time of the musical beat. For Thompson, the metrical pattern is a mimesis of the essential features of the spoken language, and the tension between this pattern and the natural speech-rhythms in a line of poetry gives us a situation in which the language is being set against an abstract model of itself. As in Wordsworth's "similitude

in dissimilitude," the differences as well as the correspondences between the actual language and the model language
give rise to the unique pleasures of metrical poetry.

The pleasures are real, and the art of combining rhythms
is an important technique in the use of poetic language,
but the listener to poetry may feel at times that such descriptions of that art seem to be strangely intellectualized
responses to the rhythms he hears. Rhythm in poetry (or
in any art) is the organization of movement, and poetic
meter is a measure of that organization. But meter—the
"measure"—can take on a life and a form of its own distinct from the language it is measuring. Thus Wordsworth
could speak of meter tempering the language of a poem, or
of meter bringing associations with certain feelings into
the language of a poem. In the case of tension, or syncopation, the listener must hear a combination of actual rhythms
in the poem with an abstract model of those rhythms. The
art of combining rhythms is here made somewhat cerebral
by the fact that meter does not exist—that is, it is not
physically present—in the poetry whenever its pattern is
broken. That pattern, moreover, is broken often in any
poetry that is rhythmically interesting. At such times when
meter disappears from the language of the poem it must be
supplied by the listener, whose memory of its past existence
and anticipation of its future existence hold up in his
mind a ghostly, patterned backdrop against which the actual
rhythms of the language perform their contrary dance.

Our concern is with the roots of rhythm in language,
and from this point of view meter is a late and artistically
sophisticated concept—"an exercise in abstraction" by both
the poet and the listener.[2] The melopoeia of song, charm,
and speech are not intellectualized concepts but old forces
in language directed at the ear, or rather at the body as a
whole as a perceptor of rhythm. They are physical forces
that our bodies feel, and they are concerned with power
and action. Whether meter is itself an abstraction of song-
melos or of speech-melos (I believe both versions to be true,

as well as a few others), its presence in poetry is the result not of any direct imperatives for magical or social action but of the conscious imposition of a conceptual pattern upon language. Its effects in poetry have been rich and subtle, but what might be forgotten is that the roots themselves are still present in language—rhythmical forces which are themselves capable of rich and varied combinations. Every poet, however skillful his use of meter, still seems to feel these forces actively working beneath his metrical pattern, directing his rhythms into different and often unexpected kinds of syncopations.

The melopoeia of song and the melopoeia of speech are of course two of these radical forces. New books of poems appear each year with the word "songs" on their title pages, recalling the lyre and the lute of the Greek Melic poets and the medieval troubadours as emblems of the lyric grace to be heard within. Similarly, each generation of poets reaffirms the spoken language as a source of the rhythms of poetry. For Dryden it was the witty conversation of the Restoration court, for Williams it was "the American idiom" of a decaying industrial town, but in each case the source is considered to be the language really spoken by men. The third root—less well recognized, perhaps, but no less fundamental—lies in the mysterious actions of the closed, internal rhythms of language, the echoing reflections of sound we have called charm-melos. It is the irregular rhythm of special, hidden powers in language, quite distinct from the commerce of everyday speech and equally distinct from the more regular rhythms of music and song. It can appear anywhere, in Dryden or in Williams as well as in verses by Poe, songs by Shakespeare, cantos by Pound, or lyrics by Blake. All three roots are basic organizations of movement in language, actual rhythms capable of actual, not intellectual, syncopations.

We have already heard some of this in the chants. When a poem takes on the rhythmical qualities of a chant, we recognize the emergence of an old rhythm that seems to be almost a fundamental root in itself. Song-melos dominates: the primary rhythm in the chants is the forward push of the dance beat, a regular, controlling rhythm that is originally external to, and probably prior to, the language. But we saw that the chant rhythm as a whole is a combined form, an early and important complication of rhythms that bends both speech-melos and charm-melos to the more regular rhythms of music and dance. In the Australian chant, speech rhythm gives way completely to dance rhythm; in the Navaho prayer, the charm rhythm is taken over by the external dance-beat without being entirely lost. The steady musical beat in the chants gives a regular motion to the language of speech and the language of charm, carrying them forward on a continuous rhythm through time and action. The chant rhythm, we speculated further, is a basic use of language that both reflects and directs social action toward communal goals, a force that seems never to be far away when this rhythm enters poetry. In the Eskimo dance song, in the Navaho and Australian chants, in the prophecies of the Ghost Dance and of the Maya poet Chilam Balam, and in the poems of Ginsberg and Baraka, there is rhythmically and thematically a strong sense of movement and action, a communal rhythm enforcing communal participation and communal identity. The rhythm of Blake's "Tyger" can be familiarly graphed in terms of a formal meter, but we also hear in it the questioning rhythms of speech-melos and the sound-echoes of charm-melos caught up and carried along on the steady beats of a children's song. And in such songs the deeper powers of this old rhythm persist: watch your daughters jumping rope to a skip-rope rhyme and you will see a social ritual, a dance.

The rhythmical situation in a lyric poem, then, is somewhat more complex than just the syncopation of metrical pattern and speech rhythm. There are also present other rhythms derived from other uses of language—old, compelling forces whose purpose was to move. Modern poetry has generally worked toward releasing those rhythms by first dropping the conventional metrical patterns. But even in poetry with a recognizable meter (the trochaic pattern of Blake's poem, of the witches' charm in *Macbeth*, and of Ariel's song in *The Tempest*, for example) deeper lyric rhythms are also active. The distinctive rhythm of lyric, I suggest, is actually a complex interplay of rhythms in language, a syncopation that crosses the rhythms of speech-melos, charm-melos, and song-melos. The modern poets who break the metrical patterns to explore other rhythms are working not to invent something new but to recover something old in the poet's language.

When Sidney composed his *Astrophel and Stella* sonnets in 1580 and 1581, he established, John Thompson has shown, a standard for metrical poetry in English that lasted three hundred years (*The Founding of English Metre*, pp. 139-56). It was a standard marked by Sidney's consummately skillful and artistic use of metrical tension, the interplay between the abstract metrical pattern and the rhythms of speech. After Sidney we have the magnificent tradition of the English pentameter line that runs up through Tennyson and that the finest poets of the language have made their instrument. Before Sidney, however, stretches an even longer tradition of English poetry, including a century of poetry in early modern English. The sixteenth century was a period of both dazzling and dull experimentation with the rhythms of poetry, and a period which produced, in the end, somewhat better than the usual proportions of fruit to chaff. But the tradition of English poetry it inherited was not a continuous metrical tradition. Chaucer had used the iambic pentameter line (or, perhaps more precisely, the five-stress, basically decasyllabic, line) with skillful flexibility, but, because of unusually rapid changes in the pronunciation and grammatical forms of the language during the intervening century, the poets of the sixteenth century could not hear it. They heard instead a master of older, rougher rhythms, and in 1575 Gascoigne could write in his treatise on English meter that

> our father *Chaucer* hath used the same libertie in feete and measures that the Latinists do use: and who so ever do peruse and well consider his workes, he shall finde that although his lines are not alwayes of one selfe same number of Syllables, yet beyng redde by one that hath understanding, the longest verse and that which hath most Syllables in it, will fall (to the eare) correspondent unto that whiche hath fewest sillables in it: and like wise that whiche hath in it fewest syllables, shalbe founde yet to consist of woordes that have suche naturall sounde, as may seeme equall in length to a verse which hath many moe sillables of lighter accentes. And surely I can lament that wee are fallen into suche a playne and simple manner of wryting, that there is none other foote used but one. . . .[3]

Gascoigne heard in the poetry of Chaucer the quantitative meters of the Ancients, but he also heard faintly behind this an older rhythm, a song-melos built on musical measure. And although he may have lamented that the poets of 1575 were using no other "foote" but the iambic, he was also the ablest champion of this "new" regular pattern in English poetry which Sidney was shortly to use so well.

In the first half of the century the situation was somewhat different. The iambic pattern was there in the poetry, already in association with familiar verse forms such as the rhyme-royal stanza and the newly rediscovered sonnet. But some poets worked with equal vigor in using other, and often deeper, rhythms in the language of poetry, and without the overlay of the iambic pattern we can perhaps hear more clearly in this earlier poetry the root rhythms of song-melos, charm-melos, and speech-melos. Two early-Tudor poets in particular, Skelton and Wyatt, call for our attention. Somewhat more than a generation apart, they reveal to us, in their very different ways, full ranges of these deeper rhythms. Their poems were written primarily for listeners rather than readers, sophisticated listeners in the English court who could hear, recognize, and take delight in the shifting complexities of rhythmical language. Some poems of both poets were actually set to music and sung, but more important to our inquiry is the music in their language, and their art of combining rhythms.

At the beginning of the century John Skelton was already at work. In his lifetime he was awarded laureate degrees by the universities of Oxford, Louvain, and Cambridge, he was tutor to the young prince who become England's Henry VIII, he was rector of a parish church in the small Norfolk town of Diss, and he finally held the title of *orator regius* in the court of his former pupil. Most of this he tells us freely in his poetry, and displays as well the wide and curious knowledge of an educated cleric living in England at the end of the Middle Ages and the beginning of the Renaissance. The many subjects central and obscure that were tucked away in the trivium and quadrivium (or "trivials" and "quatrivials," as Skelton calls them) figure prominently in a poetry teeming with rhetorical devices, frequent quotation and original verses in Latin, Biblical references and parables, and constant allusion to classical literature, fable, and bestiary-lore. The poetry also reveals his thorough knowledge of both the principles and practice of music. Skelton died in 1529, but he earned one further title two centuries later when Alexander Pope dubbed him "beastly Skelton," a title that has stuck as firmly as all the others of which the old poet was so proud.

Pope had more objections to Skelton than simply to the rhythms of his poetry—there were the problems which certain of Skelton's poems, "consisting almost wholly of Ribaldry, Obscenity, and Scurrilous Language," presented to neoclassical ideas of decorum—but a poet whose genius lay in metrical regularity and the balanced subtleties of iambic

pentameter couplets could not have helped feeling un-
comfortable about a poetic rhythm that probably was, to
Pope's ears, altogether too appropriate and fitting for such
subject-matter.[4] But it is that music, the rushing, raggedy
rhythm of what has become known as "Skeltonic" verse,
that at the very beginnings of poetry in modern English
sounds out important roots in the poet's language. Not all
Skelton's poems were written in Skeltonic verse, but we can
hear it clearly in these lines from his best-known poem,
"Phyllyp Sparowe," in which the young Jane Scrope inter-
rupts her solemn requiem for a pet sparrow to hurl male-
dictions at Gib, the bird-eating cat:

> O cat of carlyshe kynde,
> The fynde was in thy mynde
> Whan thou my byrde untwynde!
> I wold thou haddest ben blynde!
> The leopardes savage,
> The lyons in theyr rage,
> Myght catche thee in theyr pawes,
> And gnawe thee in theyr jawes!
> The serpentes of Lybany
> Myght stynge thee venymously!
> The dragones with their tonges
> Might poyson thy lyver and longes!
> The mantycors of the montaynes
> Myght fede them on thy braynes!
>
> . . . .
>
> Of Inde the gredy grypes
> Myght tere out all thy trypes!
> Of Arcady the beares
> Might plucke awaye thyne eares!
> The wylde wolfe Lycaon
> Byte asondre thy backe bone!
> Of Ethna the brennynge hyll,
> That day and night brenneth styl,
> Set in thy tayle a blase,

That all the world may gase
And wonder upon thee,
From Occyan the greate se
Unto the Iles of Orchady,
From Tyllbery fery
To the playne of Salysbery!
So trayterously my byrde to kyll
That never ought thee evyll wyll![5]

> carlyshe kynde = churlish nature
> grypes = griffins
> brennynge; brenneth = burning; burns

By Tudor times the final -e was generally not pronounced,
and the final -es not given syllabic value. Knowing this,
someone who listened for a familiar accentual-syllabic meter
in these lines could at first convince himself that he hears
an iambic line of six syllables. But that impression would
not last long, for if he listened honestly he would soon lose
any iambic pattern, coming upon lines that can only be
described as a scramble to get in syllables before the heavy
fall of the next stress ("So tráyterously my býrde to kýll"),
or lines that are "sprung" with two heavy stresses on ad-
jacent syllables ("The wýlde wólfe Lycáon"). He would
have to conclude, finally, that there is no system of foot-
prosody evident, not even a consistent number of syllables
in each line. It is instead the push of the stress rhythm that
is master here, organizing the lines by the beating of strongly stressed syllables without any counting of the weaker syllables in between. And if he went further, our listener would
find in general that the melopoeia of this kind of poetry
is based on series of short, fast lines in an accentual rhythm
of two, three, or sometimes four stresses to a line.

From a poet with Skelton's interest in music we might
have expected poetry that was close to song. This is just
what we get, but it is song of a more primitive and fundamental kind than our usual understanding of that form.
We do not get a rhythmically free piece whose primary in-

terest is melodic, but a strongly accented language that is influenced far more by the basic rhythmical structure of music than by melody. It is language in which the heavily stressed lines recall the steady beat of the dance and the drum, language that is in some distant way kin to the heavily rhythmical language of primitive song and communal chant. This will not be pushed too far: there is a chant rhythm in Skeltonic verse, but there are also important ways in which it is not like a chant. Other forces combine with the chant rhythm to produce a more irregular, and more personal, rhythm.

A further distinction must first be made with respect to this verse, the distinction, often overlooked, between accentual rhythm and accentual meter. Regular accentual meter may derive from the dance-song and the chant, but in English poetry it gives us not lyric but *epos*. There is an accentual rhythm in the Skeltonics, but not an accentual meter. The rhythm of Skelton's lines can often be heard as roughly isochronous, and in this sense they may suggest accentual meter—they have in fact often been read as such. But there is no fixed number of beats in the Skeltonic line, no patterned relationship of alliteration and stress, and no consistent relation (such as a medial caesura) between stress and pause—no system of "measure," in other words, that is applied line after line. We can hear that Skelton's lines have been influenced by the steady dance-rhythms of song-melos, but they are, finally, a more subtle and more complex rhythm that goes its own way.

One reason for this is the presence of another radical power in the language, the echoing sound-patterns of charm-melos which can complicate any tendency toward a simple, steady beat. Charm-melos is not in itself a dominant rhythm in Skelton's poetry, and sometimes, as in the chant, repetitions in the sounds of words are joined with the accentual rhythm of song-melos solely for the purpose of emphasizing and strengthening that rhythm:

> He cryeth and he creketh,
> He pryeth and he peketh,
> He chydes and he chatters,
> He prates and he patters,
> He clytters and he clatters. . . .
>
> ("Colyn Cloute," vv. 19-23)

The devices of charm-melos—the alliterations, rhymes, and word-repetitions—are here completely in the service of the accentual rhythm, used to strengthen that rhythm but not to complicate it. The regularity of these lines is not typical of Skelton, and they do in fact come close to the accentual meters of Old English poetry, an effect that is even stronger when Skelton uses his alliteration to bind two short lines into a single long line of four stresses:

> Some a salt, and some a spone,
> Some theyr hose, some theyr shone. . . .
>
> ("The Tunnyng of Elynour Rummyng,"
> vv. 247-48)

> salt = salt-cellar
> spone = spoon
> shone = shoes

Even these passages, however, add a complication to the older accentual music of English poetry. Old English poetry used rhyme only rarely. Skelton, however, consistently joined strong rhyme to an accentual rhythm, and his long runs on a single end-rhyme contribute powerfully to the distinctive rhythm of his Skeltonics. He could use his alliterations and rhymes, as he does above, to strengthen and push along the basic accentual rhythm within a line and to beat out the line-endings as they rush past. But linked sounds generate their own rhythms, too, and Skelton was just as capable at using alliteration and rhyme to cross his basic rhythm, to complicate its regularity:

203

For age is a page
For the courte full unmete,
For age cannat rage,
Nor basse her swete swete:
But whan age seeth that rage
Dothe aswage and refrayne,
Than wyll age have a corage
To come to court agayne.
But
Helas, sage overage
So madly decayes,
That age for dottage
Is reconed now adayes:
Thus age (a graunt domage)
Is nothynge set by,
And rage in arerage
Dothe rynne lamentably.
("Why Come Ye Nat to Courte?"
vv. 31-46)

basse = kiss
corage = desire, inclination
graunt domage = grand dommage
set by = valued, regarded
arerage = over-age
rynne = run

The thick internal rhymes, crossed end-rhymes, assonances, alliterations, and word-repetitions in this passage are also not typical of Skelton's use of charm-melos, but the other extreme from the regularity of the passages above. Between these extremes are the uses of repetitions in the sound-pattern heard in the passage from "Phyllyp Sparowe," where they often emphasize the accentual rhythm, and in fact help to generate that rhythm, but never become completely regular and never become completely submerged in the sweeping movement of the song-melos. Sometimes faintly and sometimes more clearly, the crossing reflections of sounds always present the possibility of another rhythm, one tend-

ing toward the thickly echoing patterns of charm-melos,
and with it the possibility of tension, or syncopation, against
the steady beating of the accentual rhythm. Although Skelton's charm-melos occurs within the dominating song-melos of his lines, and is combined with that
rhythm in his Skeltonics, it derives from a very different use
of language. The words that Jane Scrope aims at the cat are
a curse, a form known well by the makers of primitive
charms. The accentual rhythm that organizes the movement
of those words is, however, something different from the
private and secretive rhythms of primitive charm. We heard
how a charm, when it moves into a more public area, takes
on some of the rhythms of communal dance and song. So
here: Jane Scrope's curse occurs within the context of a
communal ceremony, a mock mass for the soul of her de-
parted sparrow, and her curse on the cat is delivered in the
more regular, and more public, rhythms of the Skeltonics.

"Phyllyp Sparowe" is one of the poet's earliest uses of
Skeltonics. The power of Jane Scrope's curse, moreover, may
be somewhat undercut for us by the feeling that the poet is
being gently ironic with the cursing young gentlewoman.
A later and more extended example of a curse in Skeltonics,
one with a more serious purpose, is "Why Come Ye Nat
to Courte?" Skelton's own invective thrown at his arch-
enemy in the court of Henry VIII, the powerful and dan-
gerous Cardinal Wolsey:

> He is set so hye
> In his ierarchy
> Of frantycke frenesy
> And folysshe fantasy,
> That in the Chambre of Starres
> All maters there he marres;
> Clappyng his rod on the borde,
> No man dare speke a worde,
> For he hathe all the sayenge,
> Without any renayenge;

He rolleth in his recordes,
He sayth, How saye ye, my lordes?
Is nat my reason good?
Good evyn, good Robyn Hood!
Some say yes, and some
Syt styll as they were dom:
Thus thwartyng over thom,
He ruleth all the roste
With braggynge and with bost;

. . . .

Adew, Philosophia,
Adew, Theologia!
Welcome, dame Simonia,
With dame Castrimergia,
To drynke and for to eate
Swete ypocras and swete meate!
To kepe his flesshe chast,
In Lent for a repast,
He eateth capons stewed,
Fesaunt and partriche mewed,
Hennes, checkynges, and pygges;
He foynes and he frygges,
Spareth neither mayde ne wyfe:
This is a postels lyfe!

(vv. 181-99, 210-23)

the Chambre of Starres = The Star Chamber
renayenge = contradicting
thwartyng over thom = overthwarting them, perversely
  controlling them
Simonia = Simony
Castrimergia = Gluttony
ypocras = wine flavored with spices and sugar
mewed = cooped up
checkynges = chickens
a postels lyfe = an apostle's life

This is more than simply a primitive curse, now: it has become flyting and full literary satire. Along with this change

206

has again come a change in the rhythms of a curse. The accentual song-melos of the Skeltonics is less regular than that of the earlier "Phyllyp Sparowe," but it is still the dominating rhythm. The alliterations, rhymes, and word-repetitions join and strengthen that rhythm, though at the same time they are still pulling against it in places, crossing and complicating it. The closed, internal rhythms of the curse *had* to change here, we might say, because here again the curse has gone public and taken on the more regular, and more communal, rhythms of the chant. The powers of this language are now directed not at magic action but at social action, at the naming and hurling away of evil through public means—outlawry, excommunication, or, in this case, impeachment. There is another change as well: a sorcerer's curse knows neither right nor wrong, only power, but this public curse adds the sense of a public morality that has been violated and outraged. The poem calls for social justice and social judgment. Like an Old Testament prophecy it aims at the cleansing of the society, and like the Night Chant it aims at the healing of the body politic.

Roughly seven years after the composition of "Why Come Ye Nat to Courte?" there did come to court the events that culminated in the fall of Wolsey. The old powers, we said earlier, persist, and a Skelton scholar provides us with this historical footnote:

> The more one studies the Articles of Impeachment brought against Wolsey a few months after Skelton's death, the closer similarities one notices between this document and *Why Come Ye Not to Court?* These forty-four articles finally presented to the King by Sir Thomas More (the Lord Chancellor) and the leading peers of the realm were drawn up from earlier lists of charges kept by some of the petitioners. In the light of these striking similarities, it seems to me very likely that the old laureate's pointed invective was highly influential in bringing about this final culmination of his

arch-foe's fortunes in November, 1529, a few months after his own death. Thus Skelton not only predicted Wolsey's fall: he apparently helped to bring it about.[6]

If Skelton was interested in the old powers of language, and it seems obvious that he was, he had like every other poet to search deeply into language for the rhythms appropriate to these powers. This too is decorum.

We listen next for the third root of poetic melopoeia, the music of the spoken language, and hear it clearly in the rugged rhythms of Skeltonic verse. Once attempts to discover some kind of regular meter in the Skeltonics had been abandoned, it became clear that Skelton's distinctive verse derived much of its character from the rhythms of spoken English. Skeltonics "have the natural ease of speech rhythm," wrote W. H. Auden in 1935, and modern critics have followed his lead. "Skelton developed this metre neither from Latin hymn nor from French nor Italian short-line, but from the native rhythm into which English speech readily falls" (Ian A. Gordon); "Skelton is English particularly in his use of our ordinary speech rhythms," and the mainspring of his Skeltonics "is the accentual rhythm of ordinary English speech" (Philip Henderson); "Skeltonic verse in the last analysis is based ineluctably upon the natural rhythms of English speech" (Nan Cooke Carpenter).[7] The word "natural" appears often in such explanations: the accentual rhythm of the Skeltonics is a natural rhythm for English poetry, it is felt, because of the naturally accentual quality of spoken English. Although there is a good basis for this assumption, we also recognize that Skeltonic rhythm is a long way from the rhythm of natural speech. Not even the vigorous people of England's ebullient sixteenth century could have spoken with quite the same rhythms that Jane Scrope uses against Gib the cat or that Skelton himself uses against Wolsey. The speech-melos of Skelton's powerfully vernacular, colloquial, vulgar voice is heard throughout his poetry, and it is an important power

in his Skeltonics, but it is not, I would say, the sole basis
of their rhythms. Rather it is another power, one power
among three, and it is syncopated against the rhythms of
song-melos and the rhythms of charm-melos. Like the latter,
it often crosses the primary accentual rhythm, introducing
irregularity and complicating any tendency toward a steady,
chanting song-melos.

We can admire Skelton's ear for speech when, in a poem
not primarily in Skeltonics, he catches the rhythm of how
people talk and gossip at court:

> For ye said, that he said, that I said, wote ye what?
> ("Against Venemous Tongues")

But when he combines the rhythms of speech with the other
rhythms of his full Skeltonics we hear something more re-
markable:

> Than thyder came dronken Ales;
> And she was full of tales,
> Of tydynges in Wales,
> And of sainct James in Gales,
> And of the Portyngales;
> Wyth, Lo, gossyp, I wys,
> Thus and thus it is,
> There hath ben great war
> Betwene Temple Bar
> And the Crosse in Chepe,
> And there came an hepe
> Of mylstones in a route:
> She speketh thus in her snout,
> Snevelyng in her nose,
> As thoughe she had the pose;
> Lo, here is an olde typpet,
> And ye wyll gyve me a syppet
> Of your stale ale,
> God sende you good sale!

And as she was drynkynge,
She fyll in a wynkynge
Wyth a barlyhood,
She pyst where she stood;
Than began she to wepe,
And forthwyth fell on slepe.

("The Tunnyng of Elynour Rummyng,"

vv. 351-75)

Gales = Galicia
Portyngales = Portuguese
I wys = truly, certainly
route = disorderly crowd
pose = a rheum in the head
fyll = fell
barlyhood = drunken fit

The rambling, gossiping voice of drunken Alice repeating her wild rumors, and the voice of a narrator keeping a safe distance while he observes this apparition in an alehouse, are both caught in these lines, not in any way recorded directly but used as part of a rhythm more complex than that of speech alone.

There is, moreover, another level of the spoken language organizing the movements of Skelton's poetry. Although many readers have heard in Skelton the ordinary rhythms of English speech, we will see that it was Wyatt who explored more deeply the rhythms of pure speech-melos, the individual rhythms of a man speaking. Skelton, on the other hand, was attracted to the more patterned vernacular voice of the proverb, the proverbial phrase, and the proverbial comparison. The proverbial voice is particularly heard in his political poetry, the poetry most immediately concerned with social action, communal goals, and national values. Although there are also proverbial lines in Wyatt, it is in Skelton that we hear this voice used to direct old powers into both the rhythms and goals of his poetry. In the passage from "Why Come Ye Nat to Courte?" there are three proverbs adapted to the attack on Wolsey. While Wolsey

rules the roast (v. 198) in the Star Chamber, the poet says,
all matters there he mars (v. 186). There is nevertheless
no disagreement from the nobles in the Council concerning
his judgments, only a murmured "Good even, good Robin
Hood" (v. 194). "To rule the roast" (or later "the roost")
is still a proverbial saying in English (Tilley R144); behind
Skelton's second proverbial phrase stands the traditional
formula "To make or mar" (Tilley M48), and perhaps also
"Ill counsel mars all" (Tilley C692); the third proverb
(Tilley E188) became, with this poet's help, a traditional
expression for civility extorted by fear, as the proverb collections put it.[8]

Some of the proverbs in Skelton's poetry seem to have
been framed on popular models by the poet himself; others
had been in the language a long time. When we hear in the
same poem that Wolsey bears the king on hand (v. 449),
or that the efforts of the English troops in the north at re-
sisting the Scots were not worth a fly (v. 145), we hear two
proverbial phrases that had been used by Chaucer. The
poet's feeling that he must speak out, to catch that catch
may (v. 48) whether the court pay attention or not, expresses the poem's moral mission with a proverb that had
also been used by moral Gower. And when the poet hesi-
tates to speak out for dread the red hat take pepper in the
nose (vv. 380-81), he means, as Langland would have
known, for fear that Cardinal Wolsey become furious,
wrinkling his nose in anger. It was a necessary caution:
might makes right and Wolsey had the power to make
everything he did "right"—as right as a ram's horn (v.
87), says Skelton with proverbial irony. The Cardinal had,
moreover, insinuated himself into the center of power, the
throne, and

> it is a wyly mouse
> That can bylde his dwellinge house
> Within the cattes eare.   (vv. 753-55)

Both proverbs had been heard before in Lydgate.

Other proverbs used by Skelton in this poem entered English from the large international stock of medieval Latin proverbs, many of them derived from some Biblical or classical phrase that had struck the popular imagination. The Bible has provided popular speech with many proverbs, such as the golden rule of the gospels: "Do as you would be done to" (Tilley D395). In political contexts this proverb is usually applied in terms of a mutual scratching of backs, and English politics under Wolsey were apparently viewed by the people with the same proverbial skepticism. The poet was reflecting popular opinion when he attacked Lord Dacres, the Warden of the West Marches and a man on good terms with Wolsey, for arranging a humiliating truce with the Scots instead of fighting them:

> For the Scottes and he
> To well they do agre,
> With, do thou for me,
> And I shall do for thee.

(vv. 274-77)

The "little scroll" presented to John in Revelation 10:9-10 was both prophetic and edible, and he found both aspects of it sweet in the mouth and sour in the stomach. Many popular proverbs are based on a similar balancing of the sweet and the sour (Tilley S1038). But Wolsey, the poem says, made no such distinctions: anyone daring to present some matter before the Cardinal, be it sour or be it sweet (v. 419), was risking a sentence to Fleet prison or the Tower. Classical sources such as Horace and Juvenal supplied other proverbs for this poem, either directly or through the medieval and early Renaissance collections of apt phrases from classical authors. Erasmus' *Adagia*, an immensely popular collection of Greek and Latin sayings, first appeared in 1500 and probably gave the poet this insight into how Wolsey, in spite of his well-catalogued faults, could have managed to gain such autocratic power in England:

But have ye nat harde this,
How an one eyed man is
Well syghted when
He is amonge blynde men?

(vv. 529-32)

"Why Come Ye Nat to Courte?" was written in late 1522
and early 1523, when England had once again become involved in a Continental war. The popular resentment
against Wolsey's increasingly heavy taxation to support these
foreign adventures allowed Skelton to speak for the people
in the voice of the people. The poet was attacking not simply Wolsey but the bad effects of a bad ruler on the life
of a nation. The heavy taxation, Skelton says, has "wrung
us on the males" ("purses," v. 75). The workers, artisans,
and merchants of England have been forced to pay and
pay more for Wolsey's insatiable thirst for money, a thirst
that would dry up the streams of nine kings' realms (vv.
954-55) and that is turning England into a waste land. The
good reason and skill which should control government
policy have been left to roast a stone (v. 109), to labor in
vain against the reckless wasting and spending that have
left England nearly destitute:

Our talwod is all brent,
Our fagottes are all spent,
We may blowe at the cole. (vv. 79-81)

Opportunities have been let slip by, and "There went the
hare away" (v. 117). Once the war with France began,
Scotland attacked England from the north, and the poet
saw the blight spreading out from the Lord Chancellor
weakening the defense of English soil: the English forces,
he says, have their hearts in their hose (v. 286), and the
Scots make fools of them, make them peel straws (v. 262).
To add insult to injury, Wolsey has with hypocritical
righteousness closed the Southwark brothel known by the

sign of "The Cardinal's Hat," driving out the girls and customers with the insulting proverbial phrase "Wyll ye bere no coles?" (v. 240). This from a man whose scorn for the commandments of his own religion, Skelton later points out, would make the devil sweat (v. 1085).

The poem, then, was not simply a personal attack but a public action. Wolsey's dangerously erratic power—he would as soon smite his friend as his foe (vv. 579-80)—was a threat to the entire nation, and his power over the young king an usurpation of the right and the natural. Skelton even suggested that Wolsey used sorcery over the king (a traditional charge directed at powerful ministers), and he prayed that God would open the king's eyes, would grant him the grace to know the falcon from the crow, the wolf from the lamb (vv. 772-73), and to know that the grey goose was no swan (v. 886). But since another venerable proverb told him that God helps those who help themselves, he did more than pray, and in his poem we hear the old tutor's contributions to more immediate action.[9]

The popular wisdom of the proverb was one instrument in that action, and the speech patterns of the proverb fit easily into the rhythms of Skeltonic verse. Rhythm, we noted earlier, is the organization of movement, and the proverb is a step already taken by the popular idiom toward the rhythmical organization of language. It is a rhythmical unit based on speech. Among native English proverbs, or foreign proverbs that have been adapted to English speech, we find many that have been further organized into more formal patterns of rhythm. Although the proverb is too short for sustained song-melos, many proverbs show a rudimentary accentual rhythm of the sort called "dipodic." Some have gone further yet and have taken on the additional rhythmical organization of sound-repetitions, with alliterations ("To rule the roast," "Sweet meat will have sour sauce"), rhymes ("Let them that be cold blow at the coal," "Their thrift waxes thin that spend more than they win"), and word-repetitions ("Catch that catch may," "Will

will have will though will woe win"). The folk poetry of these proverbs could be adapted, often with little or no change, to the rhythms of the Skeltonics. In "Why Come Ye Nat to Courte?" Skelton used the communal voice of this popular idiom to pour contempt on what he and the people saw as an unfit man recklessly controlling the country, to point out and to protest such a ruler's many violations of the common good, and to warn of the dangers— political, economic, and moral—that befall a land when a man who rules neither by virtue of nobility nor by popular assent gathers all the power into his ambitious hands. Although four centuries have swept away the events that occasioned this very political poem, it has deep roots. Its purpose was, and is, to move, and its instruments are the whole battery of rhythms in language that have always been directed at action.

By the middle of the sixteenth century the iambic pentameter pattern had become solidly established as the standard basis for the music of English poetry, and by the end of the century Skelton was being parodied. The new music first had to be learned, and for a while we hear English poets following the unstress-stress pattern and counting their syllables with the dogged regularity of music students with their metronomes. As the new pattern gradually became instinctive it was used with increasing skill and flexibility; at the same time, it appears, the feeling grew that there was something embarrassing and uncomfortably unsophisticated, something of the country hayseed and rustic buffoonery, in the older music of Skelton's poetry. In the iambic pentameter context of Robert Greene's play *Friar Bacon and Friar Bungay* (ca. 1589), we hear the old rhythms mocked in several of the speeches of Miles, Friar Bacon's poor-scholar. Miles is a bungler and a clown who usually speaks in prose, but when he is caught in a drunken brawl by a constable or when he must address nobility he breaks out into verse that parodies Skelton's rhythms and constant

Latinizing. Here he sets the table for Bacon's royal dinner-guests:

Salvete, omnes reges,   that govern your *greges,*
In Saxony and Spain,   in England and in Almain;
For all this frolic rable   must I cover thee, table,
With trenchers, salt, and cloth,   and then look for
   your broth.

In an age that valued regular meter the rough native music of Skelton's poetry—the accentual rhythms of his song-melos, his charm-melos drawn from the sounds of English words, his speech-melos of the English proverbial voice—were out of fashion and had become simply doggerel.

This was a recurring response to Skelton's poetry up through the nineteenth century, but it is a response we are now in a good position to challenge. We have been listening to rhythmic roots in the language of a poet working just before the establishment of the iambic pattern in English. Skelton's poetry, though not oral poetry in terms of its composition, was unequivocally poetry that was meant to be heard, and what his contemporaries must have heard in listening to these poems was not in any way simple poetry, not doggerel, but poetry built on the shifting combinations of various radical rhythms. Doggerel is verse without these complexities of rhythmical organization, and in Skelton's complexity, in the different levels of rhythms going on simultaneously, we hear far more than we hear in the simple rhythms of "light" verse such as limericks or Yukon poetry. For the later sixteenth century, and for several centuries afterward, doggerel meant irregular verse. For us doggerel is more often verse that is too regular, an obvious thought carried by an obvious rhythm. There is perfect iambic pentameter doggerel as well as mock-Skeltonic doggerel. It is, we might say, poetry that has lost its roots and is left with only a single, mechanical pattern for its rhythmical base. To this one monotonously regular principle are sacrificed any of the complicating effects of melopoeia. The rhythms of speech and the cross-rhythms of alliterations and rhymes are, along with meaning itself, made to fit a ready-made pattern. Skelton's heavy, accentual rhythms, his "filler" rhymes, and his closeness to the rhythms of popular poetry do lead him at times close to doggerel, but a good poet can safely flirt with rhythms that poets with less control should avoid. In Skelton's best passages we hear the syncopation of rhythms derived from song and dance, from charm, and from speech. The accentual rhythm and rushing movement of song-melos dominate, but charm-melos and speech-melos are there to add their complications. It is his art of combining rhythms that first of all saves Skelton from doggerel.

When Robert Greene describes in neatly end-stopped iambic pentameter lines a royal drinking party and a royal infatuation, the excitement and energy of the event is rhythmically carried by the substitution of three initial trochees for iambs:

> After the Prince got to the keeper's lodge
> And had been jocund in the house a while,
> Tossing of ale and milk in country cans,
> Whether it was the country's sweet content,
> Or else the bonny damsel fill'd us drink,
> That seem'd so stately in her stammel red,
> Or that a qualm did cross his stomach then,
> But straight he fell into his passions.
>
> (*Friar Bacon and Friar Bungay*)

When Skelton describes a drinking bout, one taking place on a very different level of society, we can hear another kind of control at work as he consciously and deliberately comes close to doggerel verse but once again escapes:

> But to make up my tale,
> She breweth noppy ale,
> And maketh therof port sale

To travellars, to tynkers,
To sweters, to swynkers,
And all good ale drynkers,
That wyll nothynge spare,
But drynke tyll they stare
And brynge themselfe bare,
With, Now away the mare,
And let us sley care,
As wyse as an hare!
("The Tunnyng of Elynour Rummyng,"
vv. 101-12)

noppy = nappy
port sale = public sale
sweters = sweaters
swynkers = laborers
sley = slay

It was probably this poem more than any other that prompted Pope's "beastly Skelton." The swinging accentual rhythm and the conspicuous rhymes and alliterations do suggest an intentional use of doggerel and popular verse for this rollicking account of midday drinkers in Elinour Rumming's ale house. Yet even here the rhythms are not that simple. The rushing movement of Skelton's song-melos again dominates, with the alliterations and rhymes used to emphasize its basic two-beat rhythm. But they cross that rhythm, too, echoing back and forth with the energy of drunken games and generating rhythms of their own even while they are pushing forward and strengthening the beat. And through the pounding stress-rhythm also wind the rhythms of speech: we hear the narrator's voice commenting on the scene even while it is trying to keep up with the confused bustle, the voices of the crowding customers greeting and toasting each other in shouting euphoria, and the popular voice of the three proverbial sayings ending the passage. Each voice brings with it a distinctive rhythmic movement of its own at the same time it fits into the wildly dancing rhythm of the poem's Skeltonics.

This leads us, finally, to one further quality that distinguishes the poetry of Skelton and its curious rhythms from doggerel verse. Doggerel forces language and meaning down under a rhythmical cliché, but melopoeia charges the words of a poem, as Pound said, "over and above their plain meaning, with some musical property, which directs the bearing or trend of that meaning." Pound was not concerned here with onomatopoeic rhythm, for rhythm has no lexical meaning to add to the "plain meaning" of the words. He was concerned with rhythm as an action in language, and we have heard in Skelton's poetry language directed and informed by such rhythmical actions. Because the accentual song-melos dominates Skelton's rhythms, what we hear most is language charged with the social actions of the chant rhythm, and correspondingly little of the secretive, magical actions of the charm rhythm. A passage from a requiem mass attended by all the birds in the bestiaries calls down upon their common enemy the just punishments of vivid disasters, and the words are directed by the old rhythmical actions of communal chant and public curse. A poem about women drinking together moves with the fast-paced rhythms of ale-house conviviality, the words charged with the social rhythms of a communal celebration. A political poem attacking an unhealthy influence in the nation calls with the song-melos of dance and drum for social action, again transforms the private charm-melos of a curse into a public power, and with the patterned speech-melos of proverbial sayings adds to the poet's personal indictment the voice of popular judgment.

Literary history has decided that Skelton is a minor poet, and the close attention that we have given to the radical rhythms in some of his poetry might seem to be a case of over-subtle analysis employed on essentially crude material. Although the analysis itself should suggest that any such judgments miss the complexities of one of our most vigorous poets, there are further reasons why Skelton is especially valuable for hearing the melopoeia of English poetry. He composed his poems when poetry was still meant to be heard more than seen, a fundamental premise of poetry that the spread of printing was soon to change; he was a poet who knew music and who had a musician's ear for combining rhythms; he worked with rhythms in the English language at a time just before the iambic metrical pattern became the standard music for English poetry. He is most valuable to us, finally, because he reveals the roots of his rhythms and allows us to separate in analysis things that actually happen together in the language of poetry.

For the roots come together in poetry, generating rhythms that cross and interfere with each other, reinforcing or dampening each other as they do. Song-melos, as we have used the term, is derived from the pure rhythm of a regular, physical pulse, and it is theoretically prior to language. When it enters language, however, and eventually leaves the drum and the dance behind, it must use features in the language itself to mark the beat. It does this in English poetry by sounding out a stressed syllable at regular intervals, but this physical push behind a syllable also brings out the sound-quality of the syllable so that it echoes back and forth across the poem, connects with similar sounds, and generates the rhythms and sound-patterns of charm-melos. Conversely, the rhymes, alliterations, and other sound-repetitions of charm-melos set up rhythms that can be regularly patterned in such a way that they strengthen or in fact generate the regular pulsations of song-melos. The rhythms of the spoken language, furthermore, can also be arranged so that they generate a rudimentary song-melos or a simple pattern of charm-melos, as we heard in the "dipodic" rhythms and basic rhymes of some proverbs. Yet, though these rhythms do happen together, and set up many levels of mutual reactions as they do, our basic assumption as we listen to them is that they are at root different rhythms derived from different uses of language. In Skelton we can still hear uses of language that go back to the rhythms of the communal chant, the rhythms of a primitive curse, and the rhythms of the *vox populi*, roots which become more difficult to trace in poets who weave their rhythmical strands more finely. Centuries later Gerard Manley Hopkins felt his way back to the same roots that charge the language of Skelton's poetry. Hopkins was another poet seriously interested in music, and he insisted again and again that his poetry must be heard aloud rather than silently read. His "sprung rhythm" is a counterpoint, as in Skelton, of our three radical rhythms, though the final result is quite different from the music of the Skeltonics. In his comments on sprung rhythm Hopkins concentrated on its song-melos, the accentual rhythm that moves poems like "The Windhover," "Hurrahing in Harvest," and "Carrion Comfort" with a heavily rushing tempo. He saw the relationship of accentual rhythm in poetry to the regular rhythmical beat in music, and he devised notations for scoring the movements of that rhythm in his poems. As a musician, he came close to thinking of his poetic rhythm in terms of isochronous measures, each measure beginning with a strongly stressed syllable and lasting until the next strong stress; he also tried in most sprung-rhythm poems to keep a fixed number of stresses, and therefore of measures, in each line. Yet he never quite committed himself to the complete subordination of language to music. In sprung rhythm, he wrote, "the feet are assumed to be equally long *or strong* and their seeming inequality is made up by pause *or stressing*," and his qualifications (which I have italicized) move rhythm from the metronome to something more irregular and more complex. When we listen to the poems we in fact never quite hear a regular and continuous musical measure—and we certainly do not hear, some enthusiastic comments by both Hopkins and his critics to the contrary, the regular accentual meters of Old English *epos*.[10] As in the Skeltonics, the sprung rhythm of Hopkins' poems is an accentual rhythm but not accentual meter. Once again there are other rhythms which also organize the movements of the language and which challenge, cross, and complicate what would be by itself too rigid a rhythm for lyric poetry.

Hopkins writes in his "Author's Preface" that sprung rhythm "is the rhythm of all but the most monotonously regular music, so that in the words of choruses and refrains and in songs written closely to music it arises." He also mentions the rhythm of nursery rhymes, poetry in which the words are not sung to a melody but are nevertheless made to follow a music we all know, the steady rhythm of a bouncing knee. But at the same time he says that sprung rhythm is also "the rhythm of common speech," and it appears as well in "weather saws," or proverbial speech. In a letter to Robert Bridges he spells out the combined nature of sprung rhythm:

> Why do I employ sprung rhythm at all? Because it is the nearest to the rhythm of prose, that is the native and natural rhythm of speech, the least forced, the most rhetorical and emphatic of all possible rhythms, combining, as it seems to me, opposite and, one wd. have thought, incompatible excellences, markedness of rhythm—that is rhythm's self—and naturalness of expression. . . .[11]

(Only poets, it seems, can get away with equating the rhythms of speech with the rhythms of written prose as we have seen both Hopkins and Wordsworth do.) Sprung rhythm, then, is a combination of at least two radical rhythms, rhythms which at first seem opposite and incompatible—speech-melos ("the native and natural rhythm of speech")—and the strongly marked beat of song-melos ("rhythm's self").

Of the third root of poetic melopoeia Hopkins appears to say nothing, but it is written large throughout his poetry in the alliterations, assonances, internal rhymes, and word-repetitions that echo back and forth across the beating rhythms of his song-melos and the rhetorical rhythms of his speech-melos. Like Skelton, he can use the sound-repetitions of charm-melos either to mark and strengthen the pushing movement of his accentual rhythm or to cross that rhythm—creating a rhythmical ambiguity by alliterating on an unstressed syllable, for example, or creating thick *patterns* of sound which slow down the forward movement of the accentual beat. Thus in the opening lines of "The Windhover":

> I caught this morning morning's minion, king-
>   dom of daylight's dauphin, dapple-dawn-drawn Fal-
>   con, in his riding
> Of the rolling level underneath him steady air, and
>   striding
> High there . . .

Marshall McLuhan hears patterns of assonance and alliteration which, rather than emphasizing the forward movement of the beat, are held in a poised "hovering"—analogous, he goes on to suggest (and here we part company for a while), to the suspended movement of the precisely etched falcon.[12] Far more than Skelton, Hopkins uses the sound-echoes in words to generate the irregular rhythms of charm-melos. We heard most of all in Skelton the social actions of the chant rhythm, and correspondingly little of the secretive, magical actions of the charm rhythm. In Hopkins the thicker sound-patterns of charm-melos generate a more irregular and discontinuous rhythm, and we hear more of the private rhythms of "verbal missiles," more of the personal voice directed toward magic action. Geoffrey Hartman has remarked on the "vocative" style of Hopkins' poetry; it is, like a prayer, like a charm, a "calling."[13]

Since sprung rhythm combines all three roots of melopoeia, why would Hopkins say, as he did say in the "Author's Preface," that it cannot be counterpointed? It was a conclusion that followed from his initial definitions. In his comments on rhythm he first had to make the large distinction, as we did at the beginning of this chapter, between poetry that uses a regular metrical pattern ("running rhythm," as he called it) and poetry that does not use regular meter ("sprung rhythm"). He then defined "counterpoint" as "the superinducing or *mounting* of a new rhythm" upon the basic metrical pattern so that "two rhythms are in some manner running at once." In the quantitative meters of Latin poetry or in the accentual-syllabic meters of English poetry counterpoint arises whenever a "new rhythm" (he did not limit it, as most critics now do, to speech rhythm only) is set up against the established meter of the poem. Since sprung rhythm does not have a continuous metrical pattern, by definition it cannot be counterpointed. One does not win this kind of argument with a Jesuit, and we will now abandon the term—still confident, however, that we hear in sprung rhythm the combined rhythms of song-melos, charm-melos, and speech-melos in some manner running at once, as the garrulous parson of Diss showed us they could.

While Skelton was working on "Why Come Ye Nat to Courte?" a much younger poet was spending his first year at court, beginning the turbulent career of a courtier and diplomat in the service of Henry VIII. The poetry of Sir Thomas Wyatt shows that another generation of poetry had arrived at court as well, one freshly inspired by the conventions of French, Petrarchan, and Chaucerian poetry of courtly love. George Puttenham, looking back from his Elizabethan vantage point, called these poets "a new company of courtly makers" and wrote that "they greatly pollished our rude & homely maner of vulgar Poesie from that it had bene before, and for that cause may justly be sayd the first reformers of our English meetre and stile."[14] The rhythms of metrically regular poetry had also arrived with this new generation, and the verse of Surrey, Wyatt's younger contemporary, for the most part conspicuously follows the iambic pattern. The rhythms of Wyatt's poems, however, often do not; there is by metrical standards a "roughness" to them that was long regarded as the somewhat fumbling attempts of a poet in a transition zone trying to find his way toward the smooth regularity later accomplished by Surrey. One of the developments of modern criticism has been a revaluation of that roughness in the rhythms of Wyatt's poetry. There are enough metrically regular lines to show that he could write smoothly patterned iambics whenever he wanted to, and enough other rhythms in his poetry to show that he saw no reason to limit the language of poetry to one rhythmical principle. We can recognize in these other rhythms our three radical powers of melopoeia, powers which run deep in Wyatt's poetry and are often much stronger forces in organizing the movement of his language than an abstract pattern of meter.

One of them is the radical rhythm of speech-melos, the rhythm of the speaking voice. The fundamental unit of speech-melos is the spoken phrase, and a study by D. W. Harding has demonstrated that in Wyatt a line of poetry will often be made up of from one to three, and occasionally more, of these basic rhythmical units—separated, as in speech, by a brief pause. Thus much of Wyatt's poetry, Harding shows, is "pausing verse" rather than the continuously flowing verse of metrical poetry. When there is some continuity and flow of rhythm over the natural pause separating two speech units, it is because the poet has formed a bridge between the two by making certain words belong to both the preceding and the following phrasal units.[15]

These suggestions are developed by Raymond Southall in *The Courtly Maker* (Oxford: Basil Blackwell, 1964), his fine study of Wyatt. Southall also draws attention to the "phrasal rhythms" of Wyatt's poetry, and he hears in this basic unit of speech-melos the primary root of Wyatt's rhythms. "English speech rhythms are phrasal," he writes, "and consequently Wyatt's 'English verse' tends to fall into phrasal units separated by pauses . . ." (p. 126). The ryth-

mical basis of this poetry is thus not the metrical line with
its measured number of syllables and feet but the pausing
rhythms of spoken phrases. "Because the effect of phrasal
verse is created by the use of heavy internal pauses, the line
dissolves into two or more rhythmical units and it is these
and not the conception of a verse line which governs the
construction of the verse" (p. 134).

Southall's most important contribution to the study of
Wyatt's rhythms lies in showing that the phrasal rhythms
are not accidental effects but the poet's carefully varied
repetitions of the basic units of speech-melos. Thus when
Wyatt translates a sonnet by Petrarch from Italian into
English, he also translates Petrarch's rhythms into the
rhythms of English speech:

> I fynde no peace and all my warr is done;
> I fere and hope I burne and freise like yse;
> I fley above the wynde yet can I not arrise;
> And noght I have and all the worold I seson.
> That loseth nor locketh holdeth me in prison
> And holdeth me not, yet can I scape no wise. . . .[16]

Although the poem opens regularly enough, it quickly
shifts out of the iambic pentameter pattern into something
else. Southall shows that the rhythmical structure of all
these lines, even the most regular metrically, is based on
phrasal variations. Each of the first three lines begins with
a variation of a single phrasal unit:

> I fynde no peace . . .
> I fere and hope . . .
> I fley above the wynde . . .

and the fourth and sixth lines open with similar variations:

> And noght I have . . .
> And holdeth me not . . .

Completing the first line is another phrasal unit which occurs again, with slight variation, completing the fourth line:

> . . . and all my warr is done
> . . . and all the worold I seson

A similar variation on a single rhythmical unit is heard in the third and sixth lines:

> . . . yet can I not arrise
> . . . yet can I scape no wise
> (*The Courtly Maker*, pp. 129-30)

The charm-melos arising from alliteration, rhyme, or word-repetition is a rhythmical element of language not ordinarily heard in everyday speech, though, as we saw, it becomes a force in proverbial speech. Skelton used charm-melos most often to mark and emphasize the accentual rhythm of his song-melos, less often (though more interestingly) to cross that rhythm. Southall shows that Wyatt used charm-melos to mark and emphasize the phrasal structures of his speech-melos, as in:

> Yn depe dispaire and dedlye payne,
> Boteles for bote, crying to crave,
> To crave yn vayne.

In the two long lines, the alliteration first marks the phrasal units, two in each line; it can then either bind the two units together, as it does in the first line, or hold them apart, as it does in the second line. The internal rhymes of the following lines:

> Ffarewell, the rayn of crueltie!
> Though that with pain my libertie
> Dere have I boght, yet shall surete
> Conduyt my thoght of Joyes nede.

so emphatically mark the phrasal rhythms that they can be heard as the end-rhymes of single-unit lines rhyming ababcbcd:

> ffarewell the rayn
> of crueltie
> though that with pain

my libertie
dere have I boght
yet shall surete
conduyt my thoght
of Joyes nede.

The punctuation of the poem is modern, and the long-line
verse form may be the result of a scribal convention of
coupling short lines. The phrasal rhythm, additionally
marked by the rhymes, probably brings us closest to what
Wyatt and his listeners heard (*The Courtly Maker*, pp.
134-47).

These critical discoveries of the speech-melos in Wyatt's
poems are important steps toward hearing the music of his
poetry, but we are here to add our usual complications.
Speech-melos alone gives us "pausing verse," music made
up of discrete units of rhythm based on the spoken phrase.
Harding mentioned in passing that the phrasal units can
be bridged by making a word or two belong to both the
preceding and the following phrase, and Southall has shown
that the devices of charm-melos, after performing the primary function of marking a phrasal unit, can then also
bind, or hold apart, two phrases. But the rhythmical situation in a Wyatt poem can be something a good deal richer
than this—a richness, once again, that is produced by the
art of combining radically different rhythms.

It is time to listen to a complete poem:

Processe of tyme worketh such wounder
That water which is of kynd so soft
Doeth perse the marbell stone a sonder
By litle droppes falling from aloft.

And yet an hert that sems so tender
Receveth no dropp of the stilling teres,
That alway still cause me to render
The vain plaint that sowndes not in her eres.

So cruel, alas, is nowght alyve,
So fiers, so frowerd, so owte of fframe,
But some way, some tyme, may so contryve
By mens the wild to tempre and tame.

And I that alwaies have sought and seke
Eche place, eche tyme for some lucky daye
This fiers Tigre lesse I fynde her meke
And more denyd the lenger I pray.

The lyon in his raging furour
Forberis that sueth mekenes for his boote:
And thou, Alas, in extreme dolour
The hert so low thou tredist under thy foote.

Eche fiers thing lo! how thou doest excede
And hides it under so humble a face,
And yet the humble to helpe at nede
Nought helpeth tyme, humblenes, nor place.

There is enough regularity of syllable-count and stress-count here to lead us to suspect, at least at first, the presence of a regular meter. But it is very elusive, never occurring in two consecutive lines, and it is easily lost as deeper rhythms emerge from the language. Again a strong rhythmical force arises from the speech-melos, the phrasal rhythms of Wyatt's lines. In the first quatrain, there is first a line of two distinct phrases:

> Processe of tyme   worketh such wounder

and next a line of three phrasal units:

> That water   which is of kynd   so soft.

Then follows a line in which two phrases, "Doeth perse the marbell" and "stone a sonder," are "bridged" by the words "marbell stone," which form a phrasal unit of their own. The result is a continuous rather than a pausing line:

> Doeth perse the marbell stone a sonder.

The final line of the quatrain returns to the poem's dominant structure, two phrases separated by a pause:

By litle droppes   falling from aloft.

If we listen for charm-melos that is used to mark the phrasal structures, examples crop up everywhere. There is the alliteration of:

worketh such wounder
so soft
stone a sonder
to tempre and tame

the fuller consonance of:

falling from aloft

the word-repetition of:

Eche place   eche tyme

and the virtuoso line in the third quatrain which uses word-repetition and alliteration both to mark the individual phrases and to bind them:

So fiers   so frowerd   so owte of fframe

In each case, however, the sound-repetitions that mark phrasal units are simultaneously part of other structures of rhythm, internal reflections of sound which echo through entire quatrains and through the poem as a whole. These are not the varied phrase-rhythms of speech-melos but the nets of sound cast by the radically different rhythmical powers of charm-melos. The speech-melos phrase "worketh such wounder" is also part of:

worketh . . . wounder . . . water.

The phrase "falling from aloft" is crossed by the rhythm of:

litle . . . falling . . . aloft

and the phrases "so soft" and "stone a sonder" both belong

to a larger charm rhythm that echoes through every line of the first quatrain:

> Processe . . . such . . . so soft . . . perse
> . . . stone a sonder . . . droppes.

There is a wonderful strangeness in Wyatt's music as these charm rhythms cross the phrasal rhythms of speech, and it happens in every stanza. To notice just one more example, we hear in the third quatrain the speech-melos of the phrase "to tempre and tame," and we also hear the charm-melos of:

> tyme . . . contryve . . . tempre . . . tame.

From this the poet moves to more complex effects and to even stranger music. We have already noticed the line "So fiers, so frowerd, so owte of fframe" in the third quatrain. It is a line which has just echoed "So cruel" from the previous line. Wyatt then varies the "so" to "some" for two phrases, places it in a different rhythmical position, and in the next line we hear "So fiers, so frowerd, so owte of fframe" boldly transformed to:

> But some way   some tyme   may so contryve.

Word-repetitions and variations of this sort occur in other quatrains as well, as in the "stilling . . . still" of the second quatrain and the "so humble . . . the humble . . . humblenes" progression of the last. Perhaps the most striking example is the opening phrase of the last quatrain. The phrase has reached back through the previous two stanzas to "Eche place, eche tyme" and "This fiers Tigre" in the fourth quatrain and to "The hert so low" in the last line of the fifth. Words are repeated in their original positions, as far as syllable-counting goes, but with a very different rhythmical effect:

> Eche fiers thing lo!

These are only a few examples. There is much more of

the rhythms of charm-melos in this poem and there could be no end to listening, so rich is Wyatt's art. But the essential point has been made: charm-melos, rather than simply marking the phrasal structures of the music of speech, is abundantly generating its own music as well, its own cross-rhythms that syncopate against the "pausing verse" of speech-melos.

When E.M.W. Tillyard listened to Wyatt's poem "Processe of tyme" he heard yet another kind of melopoeia—not the phrasal rhythms of speech-melos, and not the sound-echoes of charm-melos, but the musical rhythms of song-melos. He remarked, "*Gutta cavat lapidem*; the sentiment is not startlingly original: but the rhythm—what a strange mixture of *The Vision of Piers the Plowman* and *Irish Melodies!*"[17] His comment implies two conceptions of song-melos in poetry, and although the accentual rhythms of Langland and the melody-oriented songs of Moore represent, I believe, two developments from one source, they are different enough to make Wyatt's mixing of them within one poem sound with an unexpected music. We heard in the communal rhythms of the dance-song, the mythological chant, and the prophecy a common chant rhythm in which language is primarily organized by the steady beat of the dance and the drum. This seems to be the root which lies beneath a wide variety of accentual rhythms in English poetry, ranging from firmly measured accentual meter to the very irregular and complexly varied accentual rhythm that Tillyard heard in Wyatt's poem. With varying degrees of strength accentual rhythm organizes the movement of epic song in *Beowulf*, of elegiac lament in the Old English lyric, of quest-narrative in Langland, of pounding invective in Skelton, of praise-poem in Hopkins. The stronger it is, the more regular its organization, and at one end of the spectrum it displays a tendency toward regular, continuous movement and stichic form. Even the irregular sprung rhythm in the sonnets of Hopkins seems to exert this pressure against the confines of the sonnet form (one of them, Hopkins said, became "the longest sonnet ever made").[18] Toward the other end of the spectrum, beyond the irregular accentual rhythms of Skelton and the more irregular accentual rhythms of Hopkins, are the much freer rhythms and stanzaic forms of lyric song—the second rhythm that Tillyard heard in Wyatt's poem, and heard often enough in other poems to place Wyatt in the tradition of the Middle English lyric. There is some, though not much, of the Skeltonic song-melos in the poetry of Wyatt, as there is some lyric song in the poetry of Skelton, but the two poets are generally taken to represent different conceptions of the song-melos of poetry.

We have listened up to now for the musical roots of lyric poetry in primitive charm and communal chant, and in the invective and satire of Skelton, rather than in lyric song. Perhaps this has seemed a bit perverse. A more common and usually more appealing conception of the roots of lyric poetry would locate them in the graceful measures of lyric song rather than in the language of charm and chant, and in personal expressions of love or loneliness rather than in the actions of magic curse or mythic ceremony. Wyatt especially has always called up this more Apollonian image of the lyric poet. He is traditionally associated with lyric song, and in a few poems—including two of his best-known pieces, "My lute, awake!" and "Blame not my lute"—he casts himself in the role of a courtier singing love songs to the music of his lute.

Probably he did sing love songs to the music of his lute; few courtiers in those days, it would seem, could avoid it. Yet it is Wyatt's poetry that brings us finally to make a fundamental distinction between the rhythms of lyric poetry and lyric song. The song-melos of his poetry, and Tillyard's comment on it, especially forces this distinction upon us. At the same time it forces us to examine in particular the familiar assumption that at root a lyric poem is, or should be, a lyric song. Song-melos is the most purely musical power of melopoeia in poetry, but it is, finally, melopoeia, an action in language, and not music itself. The accentual meters of *Beowulf* were perhaps still measured by the strum of the harp, but they are also measured by language which has taken on the regular musical beat, made it a part of the melopoeia of the poem, and complicated it with the actions of other radical rhythms in language. In the accentual rhythms of Skelton's poetry the musical beat has been incorporated completely into language—we cannot imagine Skelton with a harp—and its tendency toward a steady rhythm even more deeply complicated by the actions of charm-melos and speech-melos. The rhythms of Wyatt's "Processe of tyme" may suggest, as they did to Tillyard, the rhythms of Langland and the rhythms of Moore, and these in turn may recall the roots of song-melos in actual song, tribal or courtly. But although the musical form of song gives us a name for a rhythm in language, a particular kind of verbal action, what we expect to hear in Wyatt is the work of a poet, the sophisticated use of the rhythms of language, not music. Unless, of course, Wyatt wrote songs.

Melopoeia is, finally, a function of language in which the rhythmical organization is developed internally—that is, by the language itself. But most Western song is a form in which the rhythms of music dominate and control the rhythms of language, with the musical beats and measures guiding—from the outside, as it were—the rhythmical organization of the words. This obvious distinction has often been pointed out, but also often ignored. The situation may have been different in the Greek lyric, and again in the Provençal troubadour lyric, where the melodic line of the music followed the patterns of poetic meters and the words measured out the length of the musical notes. The Elizabethan song-poet Campion experimented with re-establishing this primary position of language in song, but in most song as we know it there is a subservience of words to music. This seems to be true of even the most successful lyric song, where we are likely to feel that there is a reciprocal relationship between the rhythms of language and the rhythms of music, and where verbal and musical pitch, quantity, stress, speed, and even sense can seem at times to be uniquely at one. Such a song (usually art song rather than popular song or folksong) has also its own kind of syncopations between the rhythms of language and the rhythms of music, which can emphasize the presence of language as an important component of the whole. But the two meet in the territory of music, and whenever there is any conflict in which one or the other must give way, the language will be bent to the movements of the musical rhythm.

Under these conditions, then, words written to be sung will depend heavily on the music, and without that music an entire dimension will be missing. The rhythm of such a song-text standing alone, we find, often appears to be too simple and too regular, for the main effects of rhythmical expressiveness, variation, and complication are supplied by the music. Now this is just the explanation that has often been given for the plain, conventional rhythms—as well as the stylized and often trite imagery and diction, and the hackneyed "sentiment"—of many of Wyatt's slighter lyric poems, which seem to require the inspiration of music to bring them alive. Yet it is not at all clear that these lyrics or any others by Wyatt were meant to be songs: the poet himself never tells us, and the historical records are too meager for any definite conclusions. This has posed some interesting problems for literary criticism. The problems are of particular concern to Wyatt scholars, but they also have general implications for our concern with the song-melos of poetry, and for the distinction we must finally make between lyric poetry and lyric song. If many of the poems we have by Wyatt were in fact meant for song, a literary critic can have little to say that is valid about their rhythms. He sees the text, perhaps senses that an important dimension is missing, but cannot hear it.

Some of the possibilities that have been suggested for

Wyatt illuminate these general points. They all approach his lyrics, at least some of them, as songs. The most interesting situation to study would be that of someone who was skilled in both the art of poetry and the art of music, who conceived words and music together and carefully tried to integrate the rhythms of one with the rhythms of the other. To find this, however, we probably have to look elsewhere, back to the *motz el son* of the troubadour lyrics or forward to the "ayres" of Thomas Campion. There appears to be no evidence that Wyatt was skilled enough in musical composition to compose music for his lyrics, or that the lute of his poems was much more than the conventional furniture of the courtly lyric. (It is in fact Skelton rather than Wyatt who shows in his poetry the greater knowledge of musical theory and the greater interest in musical practice.)[19] Wyatt was certainly not skilled enough for the composition of art song, which at that time was polyphonic part-song; the only courtly maker who appears to have at least approached the necessary level of skill for this kind of composition was Henry VIII.

A professional musician could, however, have taken poems by Wyatt and set them to music, as, for example, Berlioz set to music poems by Gautier. A version of an early lyric attributed to Wyatt ("A Robyn") survives with a setting by the court musician William Cornish.[20] In a case such as this the poet has already done his work in his own medium and has made the poem's melopoeia, we must assume, complete in itself. Set as a song, some of the rhythmical organization inevitably will be taken over by the music, but it is the composer's problem, and not the poet's, to decide how to meld the words to music and how much the musical rhythms will respect the rhythms of language.

There are at least two more possibilities. With even a slight knowledge of music Wyatt could easily have written lyrics to fit the music of some already existing song, either part-song or some popular tune. The practice is a familiar one in folksong, and many early-Tudor lyrics were also written in this way. A Wyatt poem in the Devonshire MS ("Now all of chaunge") has written above it the words "lerne but to syng yt," and a shorter version of the same poem in another manuscript has the note "To Smithe of Camden," suggesting that it was meant to be sung to the music of a popular song of that name.[21] If Wyatt did write this poem, or others, to follow the tune of a particular song, then such poems do of course require the musical dimension with which they were first conceived. The rhythmical organization of the words came primarily from the external musical structure and not from the melopoeia of language.

Finally, it has been suggested that Wyatt wrote some of his poems not with any particular music in mind but with the general intention that the poems could later be set to music by a composer. If this was the case, Wyatt was still thinking of song, and the external principles of music would have governed, at least in part, the composition of the poems. For a poet working in this way there are certain limitations that the intention of musical form is likely to impose on his language. The lines could vary in length, for the music could speed them up or draw them out into equal times, but they would probably be end-stopped in order to correspond to the musical phrases, and longer lines would have a caesura where a musical cadence would fall. The poem would probably follow a consistent stanza-form, for one tune would be sung to all the stanzas, with the final cadence coming at the end of each stanza. The stanzas would also have a certain rhythmical uniformity, corresponding lines in each stanza tending to follow the same rhythmical pattern. The poet would probably avoid any complex internal syncopations arising from a strong and independent speech-melos, and he would also avoid rough sounding and tongue-twisting clusters of consonants or other intricate patterns of charm-melos. These, along with subtleties of imagery and idea, are effects in the language of poetry that music cannot accommodate.[22]

In every case a general conclusion seems to be that good

songs do not require, and in fact may not permit, brilliant poetry. Even when a poem is later set to music, some of the verbal melopoeia is necessarily sacrificed to the demands of musical organization. A musician's setting can make a poem something beautifully new, but that is not the same thing as maintaining that the ideal form of lyric poetry is song.

Yet there remain those poems of Wyatt which continue to suggest, or request, an unheard music. For a final look at these, and in the absence of any firm evidence from Wyatt's time, we may follow the interesting experiment of Winifred Maynard, a British scholar who tried to work backward by fitting the poems to music for songs in "Henry VIII's MS.," a court song-book of the period. Wyatt probably would have known the contents of this book, and if some of his poems were written to already existing music there was a good chance that the music would be found here. Many poems by Wyatt and his contemporaries follow song forms, such as the carol, and Miss Maynard found that about fifty of Wyatt's lyrics *could* be sung to music in the song-book. Some lyrics, in fact, could be sung to two or three musical settings, and some settings fit more than one poem. Poems such as "Processe of tyme" and the well-known "They fle from me that sometyme did me seke"—poems, we would say, with complex syncopations of song-melos, charm-melos, and speech-melos—resisted musical settings, and she concluded that they were rather definitely not meant to be songs. Several short-line lyrics, on the other hand, were enhanced by musical settings, for, she reported, "The faults often incident to short measures, stiltedness, jerkiness, or jauntiness, are overcome in the singing, the melodic phrases lending dignity and fluency." One poem especially fit a piece of music so well that it convinced her not only that it was meant for singing but that she had found the particular music for which it was written. The music belonged to "Taunder naken," one of the best-known

melodies of the period, and these are Wyatt's words, which
seemed to have been made for that music:

> Wythe servyng styll
> This have I wonne,
> Ffor my good wyll
> To be undonne.

> And ffor redres
> Of all my payne
> Disdaynffulnes
> I have agayne.

> And ffor Reward
> Of all my smart
> Lo thus unhard
> I must departe.

> Wherefore all ye
> That after shall
> By fortune be,
> As I am, thrall,

> Exempell take
> What I have wonne,
> Thus for her sake
> To be undone.[23]

Miss Maynard's sensitive reaction to her discovery is also
worth noting: "this is a conclusion to which I have felt
some resistance, as no doubt others will do. For the lyric
is one that has overcome the drawbacks of the form un-
assisted, and has a rare perfection of its own."[24]

Each line of "Wythe servyng styll" moves with a slow,
steady song-melos, almost indistinguishable, because of the
exact number of syllables in each line, from the later ideal
of a perfectly regular meter. If this lyric is a song, the plain
and regular rhythm is intentional, for it is only part of
more complex movements of variation and syncopation that

would emerge in conjunction with the music. The very regular stanza-form also suggests song, stanza-form in general being a heritage to poetry from music. The speech-melos in the poem is very regularly patterned as well, and Raymond Southall points to this poem as one in which the verse-structure and the phrasal rhythms of speech correspond perfectly, each line being identical with one phrasal unit (*The Courtly Maker*, p. 135). The sound-echoes of charm-melos also tend to follow this regularity—as in the alliteration of the first line—though there is some variation here. The quiet repetition of "for" in each stanza (as part of "fortune" in the fourth stanza), for example, and the strangely drawn-out rhyme of "wonne" with both syllables of "undonne" in the first and last stanzas, introduce some of the peculiar effects of charm-melos. But in general this power follows rather than crosses the steady movements of the other rhythms. When compared to the rhythms of "Processe of tyme," there is here much less of a syncopation of song-melos, charm-melos, and speech-melos, and much more of a congruence of the three radical rhythms. There is enough subdued melopoeia in the language of this lyric to make any appeal to Wyatt's lute unnecessary, but we can also imagine hearing it as a lovely lyric song. The intricate cross-rhythms in "Processe of tyme," on the other hand, belong to language alone. Even though that poem also follows song-form stanzas (with a regular meter, it becomes the "long measure" of English hymns), a lute would at best sound trivial and superfluous. More likely, the lute would be ruthlessly reductive of the verbal melopoeia of the poem, and most listeners, I think, would feel the price paid for a musical setting too high.

Music just forcing itself into articulate speech, wrote Pound, is melopoeia, and in distinguishing three kinds of melopoeia (words made "to be sung to a tune," words made "to be intoned or sung to a sort of chant," and words made "to be spoken") he pointed us toward three roots, each with a different objective, in the language of lyric. In Pound's suggestions lie our own roots, though, like Marvell's "vegetable love," the subject seems slowly to spread vaster than empires. In this chapter we have listened to some of the melopoeia of poetic language, to the verbal music of song-melos, charm-melos, and speech-melos. We have approached the music of poetry as the art of combining rhythms, for rhythm is the fundamental power that music forces into articulate speech. Incorporating into language the old rhythms of dance, song, chant, charm, and speech, poetry becomes an art complete in itself and leaves behind the basket-drum or tapping-sticks, the lyre or the lute. Wyatt may have written songs, but we are sure that he wrote poems, and it is these that we are finally most interested in. When Valéry realized that the rhythms which came to him during his walk through Paris were too purely musical to go into poetry, he made a sophisticated critical decision firmly based on a poet's knowledge of his craft. Music has developed its own arts of rhythm, counterpoint, harmony, and orchestration, and these are no longer part of the poet's art. He is concerned instead with developing and using the music of language—with song-melos and the organizing power of a regular, steady beat, with charm-melos and the power of irregular, secret rhythms, with speech-melos and the music of the spoken phrase.

Skelton, Hopkins, and Wyatt are only three examples of how rich this art of language can be and how complex the combinations of radical rhythmical powers can become. In very different ways, each of these poets was interested enough in the old rhythms of song-melos, charm-melos, and speech-melos to leave tracks for us to follow. As we do follow them in their crossings and divergings we find that poetry is not a simple pattern, that its organizing powers of rhythm are not derived from song only, from speech only, or from incantation only, but from all the deep rhythms in language.

These rhythms have roots in action, in magic action and

in social action, that a poet can recover and use—this too is a part of his craft. At root, they are directed not at vision but at power, and they enter the language of poetry primarily as melopoeia, as different rhythms derived from different uses of language. Skelton brought out the communal rhythms of song-melos for political and social ends, and Hopkins recovered in the more irregular rhythms of his charm-patterns the roots of sacred action. We hear the rhythms of radical powers in the poetry of Wyatt as well, but we also seem to hear something new. It is the voice of the poet as an individual maker, the voice of someone standing above the archaic functions of language and concerned primarily with his art. Wyatt wrote love poems, and a love poem is at root a charm aimed at casting a spell and pulling the beloved irresistibly toward the lover. But the Petrarchan stance in Wyatt's poems is that of the complaint, an artifice of isolating distance rather than an action of magical compulsion. The song-melos of his poems has roots in social action and communal participation, in the songs and dances of courtly society and in the social conventions of that society. In the best poems of Wyatt, however, we also feel the strong presence of an individual poet working alone, concentrating the deep powers of language inward and back into the poem. It is probably not a new presence in English poetry, but it seems to be Wyatt who first makes us irreversibly conscious of it. We may hear in the roots of his rhythms the sorcerer's voice using language to charm, the communal voice chanting or singing for the society, and the personal voice of a man speaking to men. But we also hear the voice of a maker speaking to his own art— to the craft and sullen art which the age of Wyatt had not yet named lyric poetry.

IX. FIRST AND LAST NAMES

"THE SOUND must seem an echo to the sense," Pope said in the *Essay on Criticism*, and he immediately produced brilliant examples of how a master poet makes this so. The roots of melopoeia in charm, dance-song, and chant show that this is a later view of the music of poetry, for at the roots melopoeia is concerned far less with the "sense" of words than with deep and once-powerful actions in language. Yet it is clear that Pope points to something that happens in the language of poetry, that sophisticated poets take the care to make happen and that readers of poetry have learned to admire. To say that sound echoes sense in a poem is to say that the poet has involved melopoeia with *lexis*, or logopoeia ("the dance of the intellect among words"), the central ground from which poets create and the area where literary critics feel most at home. There melopoeia and phanopoeia come together in language; power and vision meet in the word. Although that area lies beyond the boundaries of this study, we may stand at this terminus and catch some glimpse of where its paths lead.

By "sense" Pope meant lexical and syntactical meaning, the "plain sense" of a word, a phrase, or a sentence. The techniques by which poets involve melopoeia with this kind of meaning are many, and the artistry of some poets reaches much farther than simply echoing the sense of the words. All three kinds of melopoeia—song-melos, charm-melos, speech-melos—can echo meaning in a poem, but occasionally they also act to set up other levels of meaning which deeply validate or ironically qualify what the words are saying. The form of melopoeia most immediately related to plain meaning is speech-melos. As melopoeia only, it gives

243

a poet like Wyatt a unit of rhythm for organizing the movement of his words. But certain combinations of rhythm and meaning are so closely identified in speech that a phrase or sentence often can be understood even though verb or noun endings, prepositions, and in some cases all the words spoken were not clearly heard: a rhythm the voice always uses to carry the words and syntax of that particular phrase or sentence is recognized. Poets use these expected combinations and also play with them, sometimes aiming the rhythm of a phrase or sentence toward one meaning and then turning the words ironically about and sending them off in a different direction.

Furthest removed from the meaning of words is the music of song-melos, "rhythm's self." But that rhythm too will often follow lexical and syntactical meaning by emphasizing and throwing into the foreground the key words (nouns, adjectives, finite verbs) of a phrase or sentence, as it usually does in Old English poetry, Skelton, and Hopkins. The radical independence of this rhythm is heard, however, whenever a poet sets the movement of its basic unit, the verse-line, against the movements of speech or syntax. He may choose to stress a relatively unimportant word for the sake of some particular effect to be gained by contradicting the rhythm of speech. Or he may use the rhythm of song-melos to foreground a configuration (or "collocation") of stressed words in a line, sometimes even reaching across a firm grammatical break to bring together in one rhythmical unit words that establish a new constellation of meaning which deepens or contrasts with the prose sense of the line.

The music of charm-melos uses repeated sounds in language to generate rhythmical units. But sounds echoing from one word to another in a pair of rhymes, a series of alliterations, or complex patterns of sound-repetitions winding through an entire lyric poem call together the words themselves, and since most poets are no longer primitive sorcerers the lexical meanings of the words follow close behind. A famous example of this kind of involvement of sound and meaning is the "dust-lust" rhyme in Marvell's "To His Coy Mistress," where the recurring sound links two words that suddenly express with terse irony the meaning of the whole couplet and with terrifying speed the desperate vision of the complete poem.

Melopóeia, then, can at times do more than echo the sense of the words. In the hands of sophisticated and complex poets it is also used to bring about juxtapositions of meanings. If there is a root of all this, it seems to be the lowly pun. Every art form knows puns—there are visual puns in painting and sculpture, rhythmical, harmonic, and melodic puns in music—but they seem to belong to language most of all and to pervade literary art most deeply. We find over and over in the language of poetry lexical puns, syntactical puns, and the sophisticated form of punning that juxtaposes two dictions (and what is primarily what Pound meant by logopoeia). The simplest and most basic form of punning is the lexical pun, two meanings brought together in one sound. It is the lowest form of wit ("to know"), perhaps, when it yields nothing but a bad joke and the listener's groan, but when it discovers that two things, two different concepts, or two widely separate experiences bearing the same name also share deeper affinities, it is a metaphor that unites melopoeia and phanopoeia in a single word. The most significant puns may be as much the result of haphazard coincidences in language as the puns of bad jokes, but some poets, following their intuitions to the *onoma* in *paronomasia*, make puns that reflect not chance but a deep order in the roots of language and a vision of archaic namings surpassing in audacity anything Fenollosa dreamed.

A good view of a poet's mind struggling toward this sense of order in language comes not in primitive poetry but in the determined punning of a highly literate and slightly crazed poem written in England in the middle of the eighteenth century. Christopher Smart wrote *Jubilate Agno* while he was confined in an asylum, and only about a third survives. From these fragments it appears that Smart composed the poem with an antiphonal structure in mind, so that in performance a verse beginning with "Let" ("Let Elizur rejoice with the Partridge, who is a prisoner of state and is proud of his keepers") would be answered by a verse beginning with "For" ("For I am not without authority in my jeopardy, which I derive inevitably from the glory of the name of the Lord").[1] Smart's intention, stated in his opening lines, was to bring together in the poem the whole of creation to praise, bless, and rejoice in the glory of God: "Let man and beast appear before him, and magnify his name together" (A 3).

Jubilate Agno is a poem gone mad among names. Smart ransacked the Bible, classical writings, travel books, current periodicals, and his own curious mind for Biblical names, English family names, place names, and the names of common and obscure animals, birds, fish, reptiles, insects, flowers, and gems that he could bring into his poem. And often the names led him through underground passages of sound to perceive hidden relationships in the divine order he was praising. Greek and Latin, "the consecrated languages spoken by the Lord on earth" (B1 6), are frequently the basis of his puns, as the relationships he found in the following lines show:

Let Atad bless with Eleos, the nightly Memorialist
ελεησον κυριε.   (B1 32)

Let Euodias rejoice with Myrcus—There is a perfumed fish I will offer him for a sweet savour to the Lord.
                                (B1 276)

Let Noah rejoice with Hibris who is from a wild boar and a tame sow.   (B1 116)

Atad, a figure mentioned briefly in the Old Testament (Gen. 50:10-11), blesses with Eleos, the name of a kind of owl in Aristotle's *History of Animals*. But the name of the owl leads Smart to the *kyrie eleison* and the owl becomes

246

a "nightly Memorialist" praising and glorifying God. Euodias, a name that appears only once in the King James translation of Paul's epistle to the Philippians (Phil. 4:2), rejoices with Myrcus ("myrus," a lamprey, suggests the editor Stead), and the first name suggests to Smart a "perfumed fish" as an appropriate offering to the Lord. The associations in the third example reach further. Stead suggests that Smart was using the Greek *hubris* as the equivalent of the Latin *hibrida* ("hybrid," a mongrel), a term applied in Pliny's *Natural History* to the mating of domestic with wild hogs. Since Noah is here one of the daughters of Zelophehad who presented Moses and later Joshua with an early claim for women's rights (Num. 26:33, 27:1-7, 36:1-11; Josh. 17:3-4), perhaps her association with *hubris* reflects Smart's severe views on the role of women ("For I pray God for a reformation amongst the women and the restoration of the veil"—B1 103). The response to this line, in which Smart remembers the neighbor of a friend, shows outrageously that English family names and English place names also share in his punning order of language: "For I bless God for the immortal soul of Mr Pigg of DOWNHAM in NORFOLK."

Punning is a form of charm-melos in which the repeated sounds or repeated words are telescoped into identity. We see that in Smart's literate and educated mind, however, the sound-associations in words led directly to associations of meaning, and rather than the verbal missiles of charms we find in *Jubilate Agno* melopoeia which uses sound to bring about seeing. As far-fetched and whimsical as most of Smart's puns are, they are nevertheless attempts to use charm-melos to juxtapose different meanings. His puns lead to many more dead ends than to juxtapositions worth keeping, yet we can recognize in them the beginnings of what becomes in other poets the purposeful use of melopoeia as a power of *lexis*. The basis for this in *Jubilate Agno* is interesting, for it seems to lie in Smart's belief that all creation had been named in a way that reflected a divine order, and the poem is a record of a search for names that still reveal this hidden internal design uniting all creation.[2] It is, finally, a religious rather than a magical sense of the word: "For all good words are from GOD, and all others are cant" (B1 85). He trusted, probably too much, that any relationship between the sounds of words was not just fortuitous, and if this belief finally betrayed his poem it is yet a view of language by which other poets, trusting less, discover more.

In the poetry of Hopkins are the fruits of processes left unfinished in Smart. The search for relationships that reveal the hidden internal order of creation was for Hopkins a search for "inscape," signs of the continuing activity of divine ordering. Such signs—a fortuitous similarity in the sounds of words, a random formation of clouds—may have the appearance of chance, but they may also be clues suggesting an underlying design. "All the world is full of inscape," he wrote, "and chance left free to act falls into an order as well as purpose: looking out of my window I caught it in the random clods and broken heaps of snow made by the cast of a broom." Casting sound-echoes and puns in language is thus for Hopkins not simply a game of chance, but divination.[3] In the poem "Spelt from Sibyl's Leaves" he finds through the sound-associations of charm-melos, and in particular through puns and near-puns, darkly prophetic meanings:

> Earnest, earthless, equal, attuneable, | vaulty,
>   voluminous, . . . stupendous
> Evening strains to be tíme's vást, | womb-of-all,
>   home-of-all, hearse-of-all night.
> Her fond yellow hornlight wound to the west, |
>   her wild hollow hoarlight hung to the height
> Waste; her earliest stars, earlstars, | stárs principal,
>   overbend us,
> Fíre-féaturing heaven. For earth | her being has
>   unbound; her dapple is at end, as-

> tray or aswarm, all throughther, in throngs; | self
> ín self steepèd and páshed—qúite
> Disremembering, dísmémbering | áll now. . . .

Through the sounds of language Hopkins sees that "Earnest" is connected to "earthless," "equal" to "attuneable," and that "womb-of-all" leads through "home-of-all" to "hearse-of-all." Evening's "fond yellow hornlight," an image of the sunset as a lantern ("lanthorn"), connects through a pun with the winding of a huntsman's horn, and the result is a line in which both light and sound fall through the evening to the west—which itself quickly becomes the "Waste." The "earliest stars" are "earlstars," and in fact "stars principal," celestial princes reigning over the dissolution of day. "Disremembering," a dialect word for "forgetting," joins to "dismembering," and the juxtaposition made by the pun discovers another meaning of the poem: forgetting is a dismembering of the dappled experience of life, and like the coming night it carries the threat of black oblivion. The pun lurking in the title suggests that the poem is both a dark spell and a reading of the language of nightfall. But most of all it is an oracle, a particularly fitting form for Hopkins' multi-layered use of language.

How much, we may ask, does the concurrence of sound in a pun discover a juxtaposition of meanings for a poet, and how much does the poet labor to find one word that contains and balances two meanings in a metaphor he has been seeing all along? It seems clear that the interlingual word games of Smart and the greater artistry of Hopkins both begin in melopoeia, in the sounds of words, and then lead to new meanings and new ways of seeing. In other poets, where the roots are buried more deeply, the question is more difficult to answer, and finally not very important. When in *Romeo and Juliet* the mortally wounded Mercutio says with a last flash of wit that by tomorrow he will be "a grave man," we suspect, because he is Mercutio, that a single sound, a single word, has suddenly doubled for him and led him to his grim joke. But when Hamlet, dressed in clothes of "nighted colour" and with the "clouds" of his father's death hanging over him, says to King Claudius, "I am too much in the sun," we may feel that the prince, or the poet, has arranged the scene so that two meanings will converge upon that one word.

The repeated sounds of charms condense into one word in a pun, but so do the paradoxical images of many riddles ("What turns without moving?"). A pun can thus appear either under the aspect of melopoeia or under the aspect of phanopoeia, and in poetry it brings both ways of charging language into *lexis*, the word. John Donne's "Goodfriday, 1613. Riding Westward" is a poem of complexly developed imagery. The speaker in the poem is riding westward but he finds that his soul "bends toward the East" and the scene of the Crucifixion. The poem presents this paradoxical image held in a pun:

> There I should see a Sunne, by rising set,
> And by that setting endlesse day beget.

Dylan Thomas' poem "In the White Giant's Thigh" is to a large extent generated and organized by the melopoeia of sound-associations. The speaker in the poem is thinking of, and calling on, dead women buried in the unconsecrated ground of a hill named "The White Giant's Thigh," women who "lie longing still / To labour and love though they lay down long ago." The charm-magic of language makes them more and more present to him, until the yearning women

> Now clasp me to their grains in the gigantic glade.

The grains of the dust of the dead, the grain as regenerative seed, and the sexual "love for ever meridian" of the women's groins are all present in the poet's word.[4] Donne seems to begin with phanopoeia, with an image and puzzle about death and life, and to come to the central paradox of a God made man. Thomas seems to begin with the echoing sounds of charm-melos and to arrive at the older religious paradox of the dead winter seed and the quick spring blossom. They meet in a pun.

Donne and Thomas meet in another way as well, for both poems follow the structure of "poetry of meditation" as Louis Martz has defined it.[5] If Hopkins' oracle is one form of poetry particularly suited to the play of language through various kinds of punning, perhaps the richest development of all the powers in the poet's language is the poetry of religious paradox. This includes not only poetry such as Donne's, which explores the mysteries of the Christian incarnation, but also poetry from Wyatt to Thomas that meditates on the paradoxes and mysteries of human love, birth and death, and imagination. Here riddle and charm, phanopoeia and melopoeia, seeing and action, come together in the word, in the central area of verbal art. T. S. Eliot, in one of his meditative descents into the profound paradoxes of time and consciousness, religion and poetry, reaches rock bottom and finds, among other roots, a pun:

> After the kingfisher's wing
> Has answered light to light, and is silent, the light
> is still
> At the still point of the turning world.
>
> ("Burnt Norton")

He is at dead center. The light is "still"—motionless—there. But then he realizes that it is also "still"—even yet—there, turning it from a dead center to an eternal center which focuses light and motion, vision and action, in a word. And there at that "still" point, the poet says, "the dance is."

NOTES

In transcriptions of primitive poetry I have attempted to standardize and to simplify the various phonetic systems of the collectors, and in both poetry and prose texts from Renaissance English I have normalized the printing of *u, v,* and *j.*

CHAPTER I

1. Henry Crabb Robinson, *Diary, Reminiscences, and Correspondence,* ed. Thomas Sadler (London: Macmillan, 1869), I, 385-86. Robinson had published an article on Blake in a German periodical the year before, and "The Tyger" was one of five Blake lyrics that accompanied the article in German translation; it seems probable that it would have been one of the poems he read to Wordsworth. Wordsworth, however, may already have known the poem: F. W. Bateson notes that "The Tyger" was entered into Wordsworth's Commonplace Book in or about 1804, though the handwriting may be Dorothy Wordsworth's; see Bateson, *Wordsworth: A Re-Interpretation,* 2nd ed. (London: Longmans-Green, 1956), p. 133; and Morton D. Paley, "Tyger of Wrath," *PMLA,* 81 (1966), 540, n. 1.

2. My collection of readings of "The Tyger" includes interpretations suggested by Hazard Adams, *William Blake: A Reading of the Shorter Poems* (Seattle: Univ. of Washington Press, 1963), pp. 57-74; Harold Bloom, *Blake's Apocalypse* (Garden City, N.Y.: Doubleday, 1963), pp. 137-39; S. Foster Damon, *A Blake Dictionary* (Providence: Brown Univ. Press, 1965); David V. Erdman, *Blake: Prophet Against Empire* (Princeton: Princeton Univ. Press, 1969), pp. 194-97; Stanley Gardner, *Infinity on the Anvil* (Oxford: Basil Blackwell, 1954), pp. 123-31; Paley, "Tyger of Wrath," pp. 540-51; Robert E. Simmons, "Urizen: The Symmetry of Fear," in *Blake's Visionary Forms Dramatic,* ed. David V. Erdman and John E. Grant (Princeton: Princeton Univ. Press, 1970), p. 166. The scheme of the interpretations was suggested by the Second Essay of Northrop Frye's *Anatomy of Criticism: Four Essays* (Princeton: Princeton Univ. Press, 1957).

3. The children's verses in this paragraph are the versions in

The Oxford Dictionary of Nursery Rhymes, ed. Iona and Peter Opie (Oxford: Clarendon Press, 1951); "Bobby Shafto" is a nursery song, and "Cobbler, cobbler" a game-song. Alicia Ostriker discusses the nursery-rhyme rhythms of Blake's lyrics, and the sound-effects of "The Tyger" in particular, in *Vision and Verse in William Blake* (Madison: Univ. of Wisconsin Press, 1965), pp. 43-54, 86-88.

4. "Excerpts from a Critical Sketch: A Draft of XXX Cantos by Ezra Pound," *Selected Essays* (New York: Random House, 1954), p. 109.

5. *The Art of Poetry*, tr. Denise Folliot, *The Collected Works of Paul Valéry*, 7 (New York: Pantheon, 1958), pp. 111-13.

6. "Vorticism," in *Gaudier-Brzeska: A Memoir*, by Ezra Pound (1916; rpt. New York: New Directions, 1960), pp. 86-88.

7. "The Later Yeats," in *Literary Essays*, by Ezra Pound, ed. T. S. Eliot (Norfolk, Conn.: New Directions, 1954), p. 380.

8. "How to Read," *Literary Essays*, pp. 25-27.

9. *Biographia Literaria*, ed. J. Shawcross (Oxford: Oxford Univ. Press, 1907), II, 220-21. K. K. Ruthven suggests that Coleridge may be the source of Pound's distinctions in *A Guide to Ezra Pound's Personae (1926)* (Berkeley and Los Angeles: Univ. of California Press, 1969), pp. 11, 154.

10. F. R. Leavis, *Education and the University* (London: Chatto and Windus, 1943), pp. 114-15.

Chapter II

1. Archer Taylor, *English Riddles from Oral Tradition* (Berkeley and Los Angeles: Univ. of California Press, 1951), p. 3; subsequently cited as *ER*.

2. P-D. Cole-Beuchat, "Riddles in Bantu," *African Studies*, 16 (1957), 146.

3. Archer Taylor, *The Literary Riddle before 1600* (Berkeley and Los Angeles: Univ. of California Press, 1948), pp. 12-13; subsequently cited as *LR*.

4. Archer Taylor, "An Annotated Collection of Mongolian Riddles," *Transactions of the American Philosophical Society*, NS 44 (1954), 356.

5. Fr. Strøm, *Svenska Folkgåtor* (Stockholm, 1937), p. 210; quoted in English translation in Reidar Th. Christiansen, "Myth, Metaphor, and Simile," in *Myth: A Symposium*, ed. Thomas A. Sebeok (Bloomington: Indiana Univ. Press, 1958), p. 48.

6. Vernam Hull and Archer Taylor, *A Collection of Irish Riddles*, Folklore Studies, 6 (Berkeley and Los Angeles: Univ. of California Press, 1955), p. 40; subsequently cited as *IR*.

NOTES

7. Iona and Peter Opie, *The Lore and Language of Schoolchildren* (Oxford: Clarendon Press, 1959), p. 78.
8. A more inclusive definition of the riddle, from the folklorists' point of view, is given in Robert A. Georges and Alan Dundes, "Toward a Structural Definition of the Riddle," *JAF*, 76 (1963), 111-18.
9. Strøm, *Svenska Folkgåtor*, p. 214; cited in Christiansen, p. 45, n. 18.
10. See John F. Adams, "The Anglo-Saxon Riddle as Lyric Mode," *Criticism*, 7 (1965), 335-48, for an excellent discussion of this and other Old English riddles.
11. 3rd ed. (Boston: D. C. Heath, 1950), pp. lxiii-lxiv; all citations from *Beowulf* in my text are from this edition. I give the kennings in the nominative singular form, even though the specific line reference may have a different form.
12. Arthur Gilchrist Brodeur, *The Art of Beowulf* (Berkeley and Los Angeles: Univ. of California Press, 1959), p. 37; C. L. Wrenn, *A Study of Old English Literature* (London: Harrap, 1967), p. 48. For the distinction between kennings and *kend heiti* see Brodeur, pp. 17-19, 247-53.
13. *The Frank C. Brown Collection of North Carolina Folklore*, gen. ed. Newman Ivey White, 1 (Durham, N.C.: Duke Univ. Press, 1952), 305.
14. C. P. Cavafy, *Collected Poems*, tr. Edmund Keeley and Philip Sherrard, ed. George Savidis (Princeton: Princeton Univ. Press, 1975), p. 15.

CHAPTER III

1. *Whitney's "Choice of Emblemes,"* ed. Henry Green (London: Lovell Reeve, 1866); all subsequent citations from Whitney are taken from this facsimile reprint of the 1586 edition.
2. *Emblems, Divine and Moral: Together with Hieroglyphics of the Life of Man* (London: printed for Alexr. Hogg, 1778); the short *Hieroglyphics* (1638) is Quarles' second emblem book, and from 1639 on it was usually bound with the *Emblems*; all citations from both books are from this edition.
3. For studies of the Continental emblem tradition see Mario Praz, *Studies in Seventeenth-Century Imagery*, 2nd ed., Sussidi Eruditi, 16 (Rome: Edizioni di Storia e Letteratura, 1964); and Robert J. Clements, *Pica Poesis: Literary and Humanistic Theory in Renaissance Emblem Books*, Temi e Testi, 6 (Rome: Edizioni di Storia e Letteratura, 1960); for the emblem book in England see Rosemary Freeman, *English Emblem Books* (London: Chatto and Windus, 1948).

255

4. *The Sister Arts: The Tradition of Literary Pictorialism and English Poetry from Dryden to Gray* (Chicago: Univ. of Chicago Press, 1958), pp. 17-29. I am disagreeing with Hagstrum's view of the emblem books (pp. 94-98) in order to emphasize the complementary rather than subservient possibilities of the verses.

5. The emblematists' understanding of the Egyptian hieroglyphic appears to have been drawn mainly from *Hieroglyphica*, a Greek manuscript ascribed to a supposedly ancient Egyptian author called Horapollo (Horus Apollo); see *The Hieroglyphics of Horapollo*, tr. George Boas, Bollingen Series, 23 (New York: Pantheon, 1950); Praz, p. 23; and Freeman, pp. 40-41.

6. For the emblem of one winged and one weighted arm see Praz, pp. 35-39, 146, 202; and Clements, pp. 25, 164.

7. Plutarch, *Moralia* 346f-347a; see also 17f-18a, 58b, and cf. 748a.

8. The first half of Jean Hagstrum's *The Sister Arts* gives a careful study of the *ut pictura poesis* tradition from the classical period to the eighteenth century; the second half of the book examines literary pictorialism in English neoclassical poetry and includes a chapter on the poetry of James Thomson, who is particularly associated with eighteenth-century pictorialism. Two studies by Ralph Cohen, however, show that in Thomson the idea of *ut pictura poesis* and the use of "prospect views" reach far beyond the mere description of a visual scene: see *The Art of Discrimination: Thomson's* The Seasons *and the Language of Criticism* (Berkeley and Los Angeles: Univ. of California Press, 1964), and *The Unfolding of the Seasons* (Baltimore: The Johns Hopkins Press, 1970).

9. Gotthold Ephraim Lessing, *Laocoon: An Essay upon the Limits of Painting and Poetry* (1766), tr. Ellen Frothingham (1873; rpt. New York: Noonday, 1961), p. 91.

10. Leo Spitzer, "*Explication de Texte* Applied to Three Great Middle English Poems," in *Essays on English and American Literature*, by Leo Spitzer, ed. Anna Hatcher (Princeton: Princeton Univ. Press, 1962), pp. 201-05; G. Wilson Knight, "On the Principles of Shakespeare Interpretation," in *The Wheel of Fire: Interpretations of Shakespearian Tragedy*, 4th ed. (London: Methuen, 1954), pp. 1-16; Jean H. Hagstrum, *The Sister Arts*, pp. 151-62; Joseph Frank, "Spatial Form in Modern Literature," in *The Widening Gyre: Crisis and Mastery in Modern Literature* (New Brunswick, N.J.: Rutgers Univ. Press, 1963), pp. 3-62.

11. Richard Crashaw, "The Weeper," *The Poems English, Latin and Greek*, ed. L. C. Martin, 2nd ed. (Oxford: Clarendon Press, 1957), pp. 308-14; Quarles, *Emblems*, Bk. III, Emb. VIII, pp. 124-26.

12. For the emblem in literature generally see Praz, pp. 204-31; for Herbert and the emblem tradition see Freeman, pp. 148-72; Hagstrum, pp. 98-100; and Rosemond Tuve, *A Reading of George Herbert* (Chicago: Univ. of Chicago Press, 1952).
13. W.J.T. Mitchell, "Blake's Composite Art," in *Blake's Visionary Forms Dramatic*, ed. Erdman and Grant, p. 69.

Chapter IV

1. "Romanticism and Classicism," in *Speculations*, ed. Herbert Read (New York: Harcourt-Brace, 1924), pp. 132-34.
2. The three principles of the Imagist manifesto appeared in an article titled "Imagisme," signed by F. S. Flint but written by Pound, in *Poetry*, 1 (1913), 199. "In a Station of the Metro" is quoted from *Personae: The Collected Shorter Poems of Ezra Pound* (New York: New Directions, 1971), p. 109; all lyrics by Pound are quoted from this edition.
3. Pound's famous definition of the Image appeared in "A Few Don'ts by an Imagiste," *Poetry*, 1 (1913), 200; this article and the article "Imagisme" are reprinted with minor changes in Pound's *Literary Essays*, pp. 3-7. Pound's discussion of his poem "In a Station of the Metro" is in his essay "Vorticism," first published in *Fortnightly Review*, NS 96 (1914), 461-71, and later included in his *Gaudier-Brzeska: A Memoir* (1916; rpt. New York: New Directions, 1960), pp. 81-94.
Pound emphasized the "objective" nature of the Image, which he opposed to the "subjective" (or Symbolist) Image. The distinction, however helpful it may be as practical advice for poets, seems to me reductive for literary criticism. The kind of seeing we are discussing is a relational process that happens on many levels; it is not linear, and it cannot be described by a "subjective-objective" diagram. Similarly, the "structure" of the Image and the "spatial form" of Image poetry are terms used to talk about what happens in the relational process of reading a poem, about the juxtaposition of different realms; they refer to ways of seeing and not to the art of architecture.
4. I use the translation of Moritake's haiku in *Haiku*, tr. R. H. Blyth, 4 vols. (Tokyo: Hokuseido, 1949-52), I, 11; all translations of haiku appearing in this chapter are from this edition.
5. *The Japanese Tradition in British and American Literature* (Princeton: Princeton Univ. Press, 1958), pp. 97-155.
6. *The Poetry of Ezra Pound* (Norfolk, Conn.: New Directions, 1951), pp. 96, 39.
7. The distinction is at times made, but never consistently maintained, in Pound's writings. It is used and discussed fully by Stan-

ley K. Coffman in *Imagism: A Chapter for the History of Modern Poetry* (Norman, Okla.: Univ. of Oklahoma Press, 1951); I do not, however, follow Coffman's interpretation of phanopoeia, which he limits (as Pound often seems to do) to the "single image," the verbal description of a sense impression.

8. *The Pound Era* (Berkeley and Los Angeles: Univ. of California Press, 1971), pp. 184-87.

9. *The Collected Earlier Poems* (Norfolk, Conn.: New Directions, 1951), p. 140.

10. "General Aims and Theories" (1925), in Philip Horton, *Hart Crane: The Life of an American Poet* (New York: Viking, 1957), pp. 326-27.

11. *Spring & All* (1923; rpt. West Newbury, Mass.: Frontier Press, 1970), p. 43.

12. *ABC of Reading* (New Haven: Yale Univ. Press, 1934), p. 38.

13. *The Poetry of Ezra Pound*, p. 124; Kenner returned himself to study the equally precise "rhythmic definition" in this poem in *The Pound Era*, pp. 189-91.

14. "The Book of the Month," *The Poetry Review*, 1 (1912), 133.

15. *Pictures from Brueghel and Other Poems* (Norfolk, Conn.: New Directions, 1962), p. 41.

16. *The Jade Mountain: A Chinese Anthology*, tr. Witter Bynner and Kiang Kang-Hu (New York: Knopf, 1929), p. 88.

17. The various interpretations the poem has been given are discussed in James J. Y. Liu, *The Poetry of Li Shang-yin: Ninth-Century Baroque Chinese Poet* (Chicago: Univ. of Chicago Press, 1969), pp. 44-46, 51-57, 207-11; the translation is from *The Jade Mountain*, p. 78.

18. *Call Me Ishmael* (New York: Reynal and Hitchcock, 1947), p. 14; for myth and "transhistorical repetitions" see Mircea Eliade, *The Myth of the Eternal Return*, tr. Willard R. Trask, Bollingen Series, 46 (New York: Pantheon, 1954).

19. *The Metamorphic Tradition in Modern Poetry* (1955; rpt. New York: Gordian Press, 1966), pp. 3-4.

20. "Pound, *Haiku* and the Image," *The Hudson Review*, 9 (1956), 571-72.

21. Jerome Rothenberg, ed. *Technicians of the Sacred* (Garden City, N.Y.: Doubleday Anchor Books, 1969), p. 385.

Chapter V

1. Lawrence W. Chisolm, *Fenollosa: The Far East and American Culture*, Yale Publications in American Studies, 8 (New

Haven: Yale Univ. Press, 1963), is the standard critical biography of Fenollosa; the passage from Fenollosa's "The Logic of Art" is quoted from Chisolm, p. 202.

2. The following discussion of the Chinese written character is drawn mainly from Bernhard Karlgren, *The Chinese Language* (New York: Ronald Press, 1949); the chapters on Chinese language in James J. Y. Liu, *The Art of Chinese Poetry* (Chicago: Univ. of Chicago Press, 1962), pp. 3-60; and Wai-lim Yip, *Ezra Pound's Cathay* (Princeton: Princeton Univ. Press, 1969).

3. This is the orthodox view. In many cases, however, several characters would have been available to serve equally well as the phonetic component of a composite phonogram, and Hugh Gordon Porteus gives one example in which the original lexicographer appears to have ignored the obvious choice for a phonetic in favor of a rarer character that also contributed some meaning to the new compound: "Ezra Pound and His Chinese Character: A Radical Examination," in *An Examination of Ezra Pound*, ed. Peter Russell (Norfolk, Conn.: New Directions, 1950), p. 211.

4. "English Translations of Chinese Poetry," *The Criterion*, 17 (1938), 414.

5. Ernest Fenollosa, *The Chinese Written Character as a Medium for Poetry*, ed. Ezra Pound (1936; rpt. San Francisco: City Lights, 1964), pp. 40-43; subsequently cited as *CWC*. The essay as it appeared in *Instigations of Ezra Pound* (1920) did not include the appendix; for other editions see Donald Gallup, *A Bibliography of Ezra Pound* (London: Hart-Davis, 1969). Pound and Fenollosa were mistaken about the character for "word," but imaginatively close; according to Karlgren (p. 26) the character is probably the result of a phonetic loan: in Archaic Chinese it originally meant "large flute" (*ngiăn*) and pictured a mouth blowing a trumpet-like flute, and it was borrowed for "to speak" (also *ngiăn*).

6. As if to prove the point, the etymology of the English word "sincerity" has never been completely clear; it seems to go back through Latin *sincērus* ("clean, pure, sound, whole") to Indo-European *sm-kēro-* ("of one growing"), from the roots *sem-* ("one") and *ker-* ("to grow").

7. Thus Pound could say that in the best Nō drama an entire play is "gathered about" one unifying Image (*Gaudier-Brzeska*, p. 94). Earl Miner has shown this principle at work in *The Cantos*, where many diverse elements will center on some unifying Image; he specifically discusses three such large-unit ideograms: the heavenly visitor to earth, the sacred beauty of light, and the Confucian "middle way" (Pound's "unwobbling pivot")—*The Japanese Tradition in British and American Literature*, pp. 139-52. See also note 8 below.

8. Similarly, Pound's "ideogrammic method," through which "rose," "cherry," "iron rust," and "flamingo" are brought together to define "red," is paralleled by the "diagrammatic emblem" in which a number of emblematic images are brought together to represent a single idea (see Freeman, *English Emblem Books*, pp. 77-78) and by the "enumerative riddles" in which a series of comparisons, all related to different attributes of a hidden object, also built up some central unifying image such as a Dutch street scene or an Irish landscape (see chapter two above).

9. *Poet.* 21.1457b6-30; *Rhet.* iii.10.1410b36-1411a1.

10. "Aristotle and Feidelson on Metaphor: Toward a Reconciliation of Ancient and Modern," *Arion*, 4 (1965), 274; Mackey is here summarizing the Symbolist approach to metaphor presented by Charles Feidelson, Jr., in *Symbolism and American Literature* (Chicago: Univ. of Chicago Press, 1953), and at the same time giving his own important qualifications of Feidelson's approach. Neither Mackey nor Feidelson should be held responsible for my own doodles with Aristotle's proportional structure.

11. Hugh Kenner in *The Poetry of Ezra Pound*, pp. 87, 204, and Donald Davie in *Articulate Energy: An Inquiry into the Syntax of English Poetry* (London: Routledge and Kegan Paul, 1955), p. 41, both discuss Fenollosa's view of metaphor in conjunction with Aristotle's proportion, and both use this sample metaphor to show that a metaphor involves actions.

CHAPTER VI

1. *Literary Essays*, p. 28; Pound seems to be using the distinctions made by the Irish poet Thomas MacDonagh in his book *Thomas Campion and the Art of English Poetry* (Dublin: Talbot Press, 1913). MacDonagh wrote that there are three distinct ways of organizing language in verse: song-verse, chant-verse, and speech-verse. Chant-verse, the rhythm of bardic narratives, no longer exists as a separate form, MacDonagh felt, and modern chant-verse (Yeats) he saw as a combination of song-verse and speech-verse.

2. Helen H. Roberts and D. Jenness, *Songs of the Copper Eskimos*, Report of the Canadian Arctic Expedition 1913-18, 14 (Ottawa: F. A. Acland, 1925), p. 494.

3. W. E. Harney and A. P. Elkin, *Songs of the Songmen* (Melbourne: F. W. Chesire, 1949), p. 15.

4. *Literature among the Primitives* (Hatboro, Pa.: Folklore Associates, 1964), pp. 122-23.

5. The Dobuan and Trobriand words are taken randomly from

NOTES

texts in R. F. Fortune, *Sorcerers of Dobu: The Social Anthropology of the Dobu Islanders of the Western Pacific*, rev. ed. (London: Routledge and Kegan Paul, 1963); and in Bronislaw Malinowski, *Coral Gardens and Their Magic: A Study of the Methods of Tilling the Soil and of Agricultural Rites in the Trobriand Islands*, 2 vols. (New York: American Book Co., 1935).

6. Knud Rasmussen, *The Netsilik Eskimos: Social Life and Spiritual Culture*, tr. W. E. Calvert, Report of the Fifth Thule Expedition 1921-24, 8 (Copenhagen: Gyldendal, 1931), p. 283.

7. *The Anglo-Saxon Minor Poems*, ed. Elliott Van Kirk Dobbie, The Anglo-Saxon Poetic Records, 6 (New York: Columbia Univ. Press, 1942), pp. 117-18.

8. *Texts and Pretexts* (New York: Harper, 1933), p. 228.

9. Walter William Skeat and Charles Otto Blagden, *Pagan Races of the Malay Peninsula* (1906; rpt. London: Frank Cass, 1966), II, 232-33.

10. For primitive curse and literary satire see Robert C. Elliott, *The Power of Satire: Magic, Ritual, Art* (Princeton: Princeton Univ. Press, 1960).

11. James Mooney, "The Sacred Formulas of the Cherokees," U. S. Bureau of Ethnology, *Seventh Annual Report 1885-86* (Washington, D.C.: GPO, 1891), p. 391; the "rough breathing" mark ' indicates an aspirated consonant.

12. Paul Fussell, "The Persistent Itchings of Poe and Whitman," *The Southern Review*, NS 3 (1967), 245; Roy Harvey Pearce, *The Continuity of American Poetry* (Princeton: Princeton Univ. Press, 1961), p. 343.

13. Roberts and Jenness, p. 15; Rasmussen, p. 278; Skeat and Blagden, II, 232-33; Mooney, "The Sacred Formulas of the Cherokees," p. 343, and in Mooney, *The Swimmer Manuscript: Cherokee Sacred Formulas and Medicinal Prescriptions*, ed. Frans M. Olbrechts, U. S. Bureau of American Ethnology, Bulletin 99 (Washington, D.C.: GPO, 1932), pp. 160-65; Fortune, p. 130; Malinowski, II, 219.

14. "Onomatopoeia is a coincidence of two *meanings* or strands of meaning, one 'natural' or extralexical, the other conventional lexical signification; concord or conformity of this sort between *sound* and meaning is an impossibility. The concord is of natural, or at least prelexical or paralexical, *suggestion* of the sound with its conventional reference."—Craig La Drière, "Structure, Sound, and Meaning," in *Sound and Poetry: English Institute Essays 1956*, ed. Northrop Frye (New York: Columbia Univ. Press, 1957), p. 103, n. 1.

15. The Na-khi ceremony was known to Pound from Joseph F. Rock, "The ²Mùa̱n ¹bpö Ceremony, or the Sacrifice to Heaven as

261

Practiced by the ¹Na-²khi," *Monumenta Serica: Journal of Orien-
tal Studies of the Catholic University of Peking*, 13 (1948), 1-
160; I am grateful to George Kearns for pointing this out.

<h3>CHAPTER VII</h3>

1. Washington Matthews, "Navaho Myths, Prayers, and Songs,
with Texts and Translations," ed. Pliny Earle Goddard, *University of California Publications in American Archaeology and
Ethnology*, 5 (1907), 54-57. In this text, the mark ' indicates
that the preceding vowel is aspirated. *Tse'gíhi* is the name of a
canyon in which ruined cliff-dwellings stand, the home of the
major rain god.

2. "While the prayer is being said, the dancers keep up a
constant motion, bending and straightening the left knee and
swaying the head from side to side"; Washington Matthews, *The
Night Chant, a Navaho Ceremony*, Memoirs of the American
Museum of Natural History, 6 (New York: Knickerbocker Press,
1902), p. 143.

3. Margot Astrov, "The Power of the Word," in *The Winged
Serpent: An Anthology of American Indian Prose and Poetry*,
ed. Margot Astrov (New York: John Day, 1946), p. 25.

4. The text of the chant is from T.G.H. Strehlow, "Ankotarinja, an Aranda Myth," *Oceania*, 4 (1933), 187-200, the only complete version of the chant he has thus far published. Sections
of the chant are discussed by Strehlow in his *Songs of Central
Australia* (Sydney: Angus and Robertson, 1971), and these are
marked with a musical notation that shows an even greater regularity of rhythm than is apparent in the text alone. For *tnatantja*
and *tjurunga* see Strehlow, *Aranda Traditions* (Carlton, Victoria:
Melbourne Univ. Press, 1947).

5. "The Concept of Motion as the Psychological Leitmotif of
Navaho Life and Literature," *JAF*, 63 (1950), 45-56.

6. *Kunapipi: A Study of an Australian Aboriginal Religious
Cult* (Melbourne: F. W. Chesire, 1951), pp. 85-86; T.G.H. Strehlow has objected to the "sentimentality" and "suggestion of mys-
ticism" in the common translation "The Dreaming" or "The
Dream Time" for Aranda *altyiranga* (commonly *alcheringa*),
which he says is more accurately translated as "out of all eternity,"
"from all eternity," or "ever from the beginning" (*Songs of Central Australia*, pp. 614-15, 694).

7. "The Ghost-Dance Religion and the Sioux Outbreak of
1890," U. S. Bureau of Ethnology, *Fourteenth Annual Report
1892-93* (Washington, D.C.: GPO, 1896), pp. 920-21; the following Ghost Dance songs are all from this work.

8. Daniel G. Brinton, *The Maya Chronicles*, Library of Aboriginal American Literature, 1 (Philadelphia: D. G. Brinton, 1882), pp. 126-67; for information on the Books of Chilam Balam see Ralph L. Roys, *The Book of Chilam Balam of Chumayel* (Washington, D.C.: Carnegie Institution, 1933), and "The Maya Katun Prophecies of the Books of Chilam Balam, Series I," *Contributions to American Anthropology and History*, Vol. 12, No. 57, Carnegie Institution of Washington, Publication 606 (Washington, D.C.: Carnegie Institution, 1960), 1-60.

9. *"Howl" and Other Poems* (San Francisco: City Lights, 1956), p. 9.

10. Baraka was accused of participation in the Newark riots, and the poems used in the trial had appeared in *Evergreen Review*, 9 (December 1967), 48-49.

CHAPTER VIII

1. "The Rhythm of English Verse," in *Style, Rhetoric, and Rhythm*, by Morris W. Croll, ed. J. Max Patrick and Robert O. Evans (Princeton: Princeton Univ. Press, 1966), p. 367.

2. The phrase comes from W. K. Wimsatt and Monroe C. Beardsley, "The Concept of Meter: An Exercise in Abstraction," in *Hateful Contraries: Studies in Literature and Criticism*, by W. K. Wimsatt (Univ. of Kentucky Press, 1965), pp. 108-45.

3. "Certayne notes of Instruction concerning the making of verse or ryme in English," *The Posies*, ed. John W. Cunliffe (Cambridge: Cambridge Univ. Press, 1907), pp. 467-68.

4. Authors, like Coins, grow dear as they grow old;
   It is the rust we value, not the gold.
   Chaucer's worst ribaldry is learn'd by rote,
   And beastly Skelton Heads of Houses quote.

   ("Imitations of Horace, Epistle ii.1," vv. 35-38)

Pope's note to the last line further identified Skelton as "Poet Laureat to Hen. 8. a Volume of whose Verses has been lately reprinted, consisting almost wholly of Ribaldry, Obscenity, and Scurrilous Language."

5. Vv. 282-95, 307-23; I have as usual normalized the printing of *j*, *u*, and *v*, and in quotations from Skelton also expanded *thé* to *thee*.

6. Nan Cooke Carpenter, *John Skelton*, Twayne's English Authors Series, 61 (New York: Twayne, 1967), p. 102.

7. W. H. Auden, "John Skelton," in *The Great Tudors*, ed. Katharine Garvin (New York: Dutton, 1935), p. 63; Ian A. Gordon, *John Skelton: Poet Laureate* (Melbourne: Melbourne

Univ. Press, 1943), p. 195; Philip Henderson, ed. *The Complete Poems of John Skelton, Laureate*, rev. ed. (London: Dent, 1948), p. v; Carpenter, p. 114.

8. Nearly all the proverbs used by Skelton in "Why Come Ye Nat to Courte?" will be found, in some form, in Morris Palmer Tilley, *A Dictionary of the Proverbs in England in the Sixteenth and Seventeenth Centuries* (Ann Arbor: Univ. of Michigan Press, 1950); and Bartlett Jere Whiting, *Proverbs, Sentences, and Proverbial Phrases: From English Writings Mainly before 1500* (Cambridge, Mass.: Harvard Univ. Press, 1968). Also useful are G. L. Apperson, *English Proverbs and Proverbial Phrases: A Historical Dictionary* (London: Dent, 1929); and *The Oxford Dictionary of English Proverbs*, 3rd ed. rev. by F. P. Wilson (Oxford: Clarendon Press, 1970), which identify the few stray proverbs not in Tilley or Whiting. See also Archer Taylor's study *The Proverb: And an Index to* The Proverb (1931; rpt. Hatboro, Pa.: Folklore Associates, and Copenhagen: Rosenkilde and Bagger, 1962); and Bartlett Jere Whiting, *Proverbs in the Earlier English Drama* (Cambridge, Mass.: Harvard Univ. Press, 1938).

The proverb is a complicated form, and folklorists have not yet decided exactly what that form is, or whether proverbs should be defined by form or by content. Archer Taylor in *The Proverb* distinguishes three general classes of proverbial speech: the *proverb*, which is usually a complete sentence and which is fixed in form ("Let them that be cold blow at the coal"), the *proverbial phrase*, which is not a complete sentence and which varies in form according to how it is used in speech ("To rule the roast"), and the *proverbial comparison*, which is an explicit simile ("As right as a ram's horn"). These are the most familiar distinctions, but Taylor himself says, "The definition of a proverb is too difficult to repay the undertaking," and he suggests that we "be content with recognizing that a proverb is a saying current among the folk" (p. 3). I am concerned here only with the proverb as a "saying" used in speech, as a form of speech rhythm, though folk proverbs often have close connections with riddles, and literary proverbs often appear as mottoes in emblems. Proverbs, Taylor writes, are based on "a natural speech rhythm" (pp. 88-89). They "conform to the general rhythm of the language in which they have been taken down," and when proverbs are borrowed from a foreign language they gradually adapt to the speech rhythms of the new language (p. 136).

9. Robert S. Kinsman has discussed the proverbial voice and political satire in two other works by Skelton in "The Voices of Dissonance: Pattern in Skelton's *Colyn Cloute*," *Huntington Li-*

brary Quarterly, 26 (1963), 291-313; and in "Skelton's *Magnyfycence*: The Strategy of the 'Olde Sayde Sawe,' " *Studies in Philology*, 63 (1966), 99-125.

10. Hopkins' comments on sprung rhythm are taken from his "Author's Preface," in *Poems*, ed. W. H. Gardner and N. H. MacKenzie, 4th ed. (London: Oxford Univ. Press, 1970), pp. 47-48. Harold Whitehall's seminal article "Sprung Rhythm," *Kenyon Review*, 6 (1944), 333-54, argued that Hopkins did use isochronous measures, but Whitehall was arguing from a "musical" theory of meter; see Elisabeth Schneider, "Sprung Rhythm," *PMLA*, 80 (1965), 237-52, for another good discussion and more accurate distinctions concerning Hopkins' rhythms.

11. *The Letters of Gerard Manley Hopkins to Robert Bridges*, ed. Claude Colleer Abbott (London: Oxford Univ. Press, 1935), p. 46.

12. "The Analogical Mirrors," *Kenyon Review*, 6 (1944), 327-28.

13. "Hopkins Revisited," in *Beyond Formalism: Literary Essays 1958-1970* (New Haven: Yale Univ. Press, 1970), p. 238.

14. "The Arte of English Poesie" (1589), in *Elizabethan Critical Essays*, ed. G. Gregory Smith (Oxford: Clarendon Press, 1904), II, 62-63.

15. "The Rhythmical Intention in Wyatt's Poetry," *Scrutiny*, 14 (1946), 90-102.

16. I quote Wyatt's poems from the edition of Kenneth Muir and Patricia Thomson, *Collected Poems of Sir Thomas Wyatt* (Liverpool: Liverpool Univ. Press, 1969); most of the pointing, however, was added by the editors, and Southall, who uses the MSS, argues that this editorial pointing obscures the phrasal rhythms of Wyatt's poems by imposing on them a later conception of the verse-line.

17. *The Poetry of Sir Thomas Wyatt* (London: Chatto and Windus, 1949), p. 42.

18. *Poems*, p. 284.

19. See John Stevens, *Music and Poetry in the Early Tudor Court* (London: Methuen, 1961), pp. 121, 132-35, 141.

20. John Stevens suggests that Wyatt and Cornish may have reworked separately an earlier popular song (*Music and Poetry in the Early Tudor Court*, pp. 110-11).

21. Muir, ed. *Poems*, p. 427.

22. This approach to Renaissance lyric is developed by Bruce Pattison in *Music and Poetry of the English Renaissance* (London: Methuen, 1948); Stevens, however, disagrees, and he points

out that the court composers of this period were skilled enough to set any text to music, however complex the language (*Music and Poetry in the Early Tudor Court*, p. 107).

23. The poem, like many others, can only be "attributed to" Wyatt.

24. "The Lyrics of Wyatt: Poems or Songs?" *Review of English Studies*, NS 16 (1965), 1-13, 245-57.

CHAPTER IX

1. Frag. B1, v. 1; quotations are from the edition of W. H. Bond, ed. *Jubilate Agno* (Cambridge, Mass.: Harvard Univ. Press, 1954), which established the poem's antiphonal structure; the many obscure names in the poem are tracked down in the earlier edition of William Force Stead, ed. *Rejoice in the Lamb: A Song from Bedlam* (New York: Holt, 1939).

2. See Francis D. Adams, "Wordplay in the D Fragment of *Jubilate Agno*," *Philological Quarterly*, 48 (1969), 90-91.

3. *The Journals and Papers of Gerard Manley Hopkins*, ed. Humphry House (London: Oxford Univ. Press, 1959), p. 230; for the "game" of divining inscape through word-play see David Sonstroem, "Making Earnest of Game: G. M. Hopkins and Nonsense Poetry," *Modern Language Quarterly*, 28 (1967), 192-206.

4. Ralph N. Maud, "Obsolete and Dialect Words as Serious Puns in Dylan Thomas," *English Studies*, 41 (1960), 28-30, suggests that Thomas was also using a Northern dialect meaning of "grain" as any characteristic division or separation: the fork of a stream, the branching limbs of a tree, or the human form at the "groin."

5. *The Poetry of Meditation* (New Haven: Yale Univ. Press, 1954).

ACKNOWLEDGMENTS

GRATEFUL acknowledgment is made for permission to reprint the following copyrighted material:

Translations of Ma Chih-yuan from *The Art of Chinese Poetry* by James J. Y. Liu, © 1962 by James J. Y. Liu, reprinted by permission of The University of Chicago Press and James J. Y. Liu.

Lines from "Howl" from *"Howl" and Other Poems* by Allen Ginsberg, copyright © 1956, 1959 by Allen Ginsberg, reprinted by permission of City Lights Books.

Quotations from *The Chinese Written Character as a Medium for Poetry* by Ernest Fenollosa, copyright © 1936 by Ezra Pound, reprinted by permission of City Lights Books.

Translations of haiku from *Haiku* by R. H. Blyth, copyright © 1949, 1950, 1952 by R. H. Blyth, reprinted by permission of The Hokuseido Press; haiku by Moritake and Ryōta also from *Silent Flowers*, © 1967 by Hallmark Cards, Inc., and Hokuseido Press, reprinted by permission of Hallmark Cards, Inc.

Lines from "Burnt Norton" from *Four Quartets* by T. S. Eliot, copyright 1943 by T. S. Eliot, reprinted by permission of Harcourt Brace Jovanovich, Inc.

"The Magi" from *The Collected Poems of W. B. Yeats*, copyright 1916 by Macmillan Publishing Co., Inc., renewed 1944 by Bertha Georgie Yeats, reprinted by permission of Macmillan Publishing Co., Inc., and of M. B. Yeats, Miss Anne Yeats, and The Macmillan Company of London and Basingstoke.

"Alba," "In a Station of the Metro," "Pagani's, November 8," "The Return," and lines from "The Alchemist," "Taking Leave of a Friend" from *Personae: The Collected Shorter Poems of Ezra Pound*, copyright 1926 by Ezra Pound, reprinted by permission of New Directions Publishing Corp. and of Faber and Faber, Ltd.

Lines from "Canto XLVII," "Canto LXXIX," "Canto CXII" from *The Cantos of Ezra Pound*, copyright 1937, 1940, © 1962

267

INDEX

Library of Congress Cataloging in Publication Data

Welsh, Andrew, 1937-
　Roots of lyric.

　Includes bibliographical references.
　　1.　Folk poetry—History and criticism.　　2.　Poetics.
　3.　Lyric poetry—History and criticism.　　I.　Title.
　PN1126.W45　　　809.1'4　　　77-72141
　ISBN 0-691-06345-1